Economic News, Sentiment, and Behavior

Juliane A. Lischka

Economic News, Sentiment, and Behavior

How Economic and Business News Affects the Economy

Springer VS

Juliane A. Lischka
Zürich, Switzerland

Zugl. Dissertation, Universität Zürich 2014

ISBN 978-3-658-11540-1 ISBN 978-3-658-11541-8 (eBook)
DOI 10.1007/978-3-658-11541-8

Library of Congress Control Number: 2015955915

Springer VS

Printed on acid-free paper

Springer VS is a brand of Springer Fachmedien Wiesbaden
Springer Fachmedien Wiesbaden is part of Springer Science+Business Media
(www.springer.com)

Content

List of figures

List of tables

Preface and acknowledgments

The present book densely summarizes and interprets the central findings of my cumulative dissertation thesis titled "Sentiments on the Economy. How Economic News Affects Collective Economic Expectations and Behavior," written at the Institute of Mass Communication and Media Research, University of Zurich, Switzerland, supervised by Prof. Dr. Gabriele Siegert and Prof. Dr. Werner Wirth.

The cumulative thesis consists of four journal articles (Lischka 2014a; 2015; Lischka, Kienzler, and Mellmann 2014; Lischka and Siegert 2013), one book chapter (Lischka and Seufert 2015), and a synopsis. The synopsis is accessible online together with the journal articles and the book chapter (Lischka 2014b) and represents an earlier version of the present book.

The articles by Lischka (2014a; 2015), Lischka and Siegert (2013) as well as Lischka and Seufert (2015) are part of the Swiss National Science Foundation-funded project, "The impact of economic media coverage on management expectations and advertising expenditures in Switzerland and Germany" [100017_130367]. The article by Lischka, Kienzler, and Mellmann (2014) is an outcome of the Swiss National Science Foundation-funded project, "The impact of changes in advertising on the media. Cyclical and structural changes in advertising expenditure and advertising formats and their consequences for the media" [100018_143395]. Abstracts of the associated articles are printed in the back of this book.

I am thankful to my supervisors, colleagues, co-authors and anonymous reviewers of the journal articles, my family, friends, and my partner who directly or indirectly supported my dissertation with fruitful discussions, critical remarks, most useful suggestions, wise sayings ("Each book is just another sequence of 26 letters.") or simply with listening attentively when I was talking about my thesis (again).

Most analyses of this book and its associated articles would not have been possible without extensive economic news coverage data of German and Swiss news outlets that were kindly provided by Media Tenor.

I am also grateful to prospective readers of this book and would be very pleased if the present findings are useful for future research and practice.

Juliane A. Lischka
Zurich, April 2015

Summary

This book explores the relations between objective, media-related, and social attitudinal as well as behavioral realities of private, expert, and corporate agents in the traditions of mass communication and journalism studies as well as behavioral economics.

Economic news not only reports on the economy but may also influence its development, since the public as well as corporate sentiment and behavior are the link between economic news and the real-world economy. Citizens and corporate agents who make well-informed economic decisions are critical for an economy and for society. Economic sentiments of private and corporate decision makers influence entrepreneurial behavior, such as making investments. Advertising expenditures are part of the marketing investments of a company and are essential for the funding of media systems.

The research goal is to answer the primary research question whether economic news affects the real-world economic situation through shaping economic sentiment and behavior of private and corporate agents. Hence, this study relates three core objects of investigation within mass communication research and behavioral economics.

a) Economic news: News topics, tone, consonance, and volume of general news outlets with the highest reach in Germany;

b) Economic sentiment: Evaluations and expectations for the economic situation of the general public and economic experts/corporate agents;

c) Economic behavior: Private purchase intention of the public, industry sales and advertising expenditures; Indicators of the aggregate economic situation.

Time series analyses of data covering Germany and partly Switzerland mostly for the observation period from 2002 to 2011 are used to assess the relations between indicators of the real-world economy, economic news, economic sentiment, and economic behavior, based on the following research questions.

RQ 1. How closely is economic news related to the real-world economy?

➔ Results reveal that economic news relates to real-world indicators but changes in a more volatile way than aggregate economic indicators. News reports more *consistently* after negative and less consistently after positive economic changes. Revenue incentives and organizational influences explain differences in news tone, consonance or volume *level* among private and between private and public service outlets. Real-world events trigger *trend* changes.

RQ 2. How strongly does economic news influence both public and expert economic sentiment?

➔ The *public* economic sentiment depends more strongly on real-world cues than on economic news. News does not have the power to shift public economic expectations without the "support" from real-world experiences, which may be caused by habituated *information inertia*. But economic *experts* rely on news when they evaluate future private consumption. Experts may *presume* that news affects the public's consumption behavior.

RQ 3. Does economic news influence private and corporate economic behavior?

➔ Although the public makes correct assumptions about developments in the national economy, economic news or expectations barely affect intentional consumption behavior of the public. However, corporate advertising decision makers may *presume* that private consumption is geared by economic news and adapt advertising activity to their presumptions.

Results are presented in an overview in *Figure 18* on page 103.

To conclude, economic news *reports* in a volatile manner on the economy but *barely influences* its development. Public economic sentiment is during the 2008/9 recession, but private economic behavior is only indirectly a result of economic news. Instead of a decrease, bad economic news may lead to a slight, short-term *in*crease in private purchase intention because a downturn is a good time to make major purchases for the public—as long as the individual financial situation remains stable. Bad news may also lead to a short-term increase in corporate advertising expenditures, which can result in a short-term increase in advertising income for media companies.

Corporate decision makers may *presume* public behavior through implicit news cues. Therefore, economic news to some degree translates "into entrepreneurial decisions, particularly investments" (Noelle-Neumann 1987, 292) but hardly into private economic decisions. Hence, economic news has the potential to influence the real-world economic situation via a third-person effect through corporate perceptions and decisions related to presumed consumer behavior.

1 Introduction

News is one source of information for the members of a society and dynamically connected to a society's economic outcome. Faced with reporting during the financial crisis, Stiglitz (2011, 23) stresses that, "Information enables readers—whether as consumers, managers, workers, investors, home owners, or voters—to make better decisions. Better individual decisions would have led to better societal outcome." The outcome of a media system, i.e., its *news*, influences a society, its citizens, and its corporate and government actors. Along with direct experience of the economy, news serves as an important source of economic information, alerting citizens to economic problems.

Economic and business news may shape private, expert and corporate economic *sentiment*. The latter was just recently brought into focus of research. Economic sentiment is found to affect economic *behavior* such as private consumption or corporate investments, which in turn contributes to the real-world *economic situation* as aggregately measured by a country's gross domestic product (GDP).[1] The impact of economic sentiment on macroeconomic development has been under discussion for decades since Katona (1957; 1951) and consumer as well as business confidence has been described as an effective early indicator of GDP within economics circles (e.g., Kater 2008; Levanon 2010; Ludvigson 2004).

This book asks the primary research question *whether economic news affects the real-world economic situation through shaping economic sentiment and behavior of private, expert and corporate agents*. This questions is answered based on the traditions of mass communication and journalism studies as well as behavioral economics. It first explores the impact of economic reality on economic news, secondly, the impact of economic news on public and expert expectations concerning economic issues, and thirdly,

1 Also business investment, imports, exports, and government spending contribute to the GDP as described in Lischka and Seufert 2015.

consumer and corporate economic behavior. These subject matters relate to four of the five phases of agenda-setting research identified by McCombs and Shaw (1993), i.e., the origins of the media agenda, the effects of second-level agenda setting, the contingent conditions that intervene with media agenda-setting effects, and, the most recent phase of research, the consequences of agenda setting, which are related to behavioral economics.

The impact of news on public opinion is a major research area within mass communication studies. The question that is asked beforehand is about the origins of the media agenda, or, in Funkhouser's (1973, 62) words, as if "the media provide a useful picture of what is 'really' going on". Whether news reflects reality has been an issue in news bias studies for decades (e.g., Hackett 1984; Klein and Maccoby 1954; McQuail 1992). In the course of the financial crisis, economic news was criticized to be unable to forecast this important event and to fail its role as guardian of democratic societies (e.g., Schiffrin 2011a). The research goal of the first part of this book is to assess how reliable economic news is as information source for the real-world economy and asks the following question.

RQ 1. *How closely is economic news related to the real-world economy?*

First- and second-level agenda setting explain how the prevalence of news objects and attributes influences what the public thinks about and how it thinks about it (McCombs 1992; McCombs and Shaw 1972). Cultivation theory suggests that public sentiment is generated by television images of the world (Gerbner 1969). According to mediatization and growing dependence on media as source of information (Strömbäck 2008), the news plays an increasingly important role in public sentiment. Research on economic news and economic sentiment was established decades ago within the field of mass communication (Behr and Iyengar 1985; Adoni and Cohen 1978) arriving at the complaint that "the people generally do not understand economic affairs" (Adoni and Cohen 1978, 68). This book investigates how powerfully economic news *affects economic sentiment* of the public and of economic experts and asks the following question.

RQ 2. *How strongly does economic news influence both public and expert economic sentiment?*

Agenda setting research often investigates the impact of economic news on public opinion, more rarely its impact on economic behavior. Citizens who make well-informed economic decisions are essential to an economy. But how strongly public economic sentiment *sets* private and corporate *economic behavior* has not been clarified yet. The economic sentiment of private or corporate actors translates "into entrepreneurial decisions, particularly investments" (Noelle-Neumann 1987, 292). Economic news, private and corporate economic sentiment, and private economic behavior may determine advertising budgeting as one example of entrepreneurial investment decisions. For scholars of media economics, one research focus is the *financing of media* companies and products that fulfil important functions within a society, such as offering information to citizens. Many media systems rely on advertising as an income source to fund their media products. Without advertising, media diversity would probably decline and many media products might be accessible only at a high price, making them exclusive to the elite (Gustafsson 2006). Hence, corporate advertising expenditures contribute to the merit good character of the media. These advertising expenditures are subject to a complex budgeting process in which the business cycle and sales play a key role (Kienzler and Lischka 2013; 2015; Kienzler, Lischka, and Siegert 2012). This book therefore asks the following.

RQ 3. Does economic news influence private and corporate economic behavior?

This question therefore links media economics research with the core research fields of mass communication and journalism studies as well as behavioral economics.

Empirically, secondary, time series data on the following research objects are connected.

a) Economic news: News topics, tone, consonance, and volume of general news outlets with the highest reach in Germany;

b) Economic sentiment: Evaluations and expectations for the economic situation of the general public and economic experts/corporate agents;

c) Economic behavior: Private purchase intention of the public, industry sales and advertising expenditures; Indicators of the aggregate economic situation.

The book summarizes findings of four articles in a broader view, namely, Lischka (2014a), Lischka (2015), Lischka and Siegert (2013), and Lischka, Kienzler, and Mellmann (2014), and extends the analyses of these articles. The abstracts of the four articles and data used are listed on page 141 ff.

For analysis, times series modelling is applied to aggregate secondary data. Data derive from publicly available sources such as Eurostat and the German Federal Statistical Office (real-world economy: national economy, industry sales), the Consumer Survey of the European Commission (public sentiment: economic expectations; behavior: purchase intentions), the World Economic Survey of the Ifo institute (expert sentiment: economic evaluations and expectations), Nielsen Media Research, as published in the journal *Media Perspektiven* (behavior: corporate advertising expenditures) as well as from the corporate source, Media Tenor—not available to the general public—which analyses economic news content (media sentiment: economic news coverage). Observation periods cover 2002 – 2011 for economic news and public opinion (RQ 1, RQ 2), 1991 – 2009 for the relation between advertising and sales (RQ 3), and 2002 – 2009 for the relation between economic news and advertising (RQ 3). The observation periods include the dotcom crisis in 2000, a slight recession in 2003/4, the financial crises following the subprime crisis from 2007 onwards, and a severe recession in 2008/9 in Germany followed by the Euro crisis (see e.g. Schirwitz 2009; Statistisches Bundesamt 2012; Räth 2009 for definitions of recession periods in Germany).[2] The data frequency is monthly (economic news, public opinion) or quarterly (economic expert opinion, advertising-sales relation). The population comprises the main public-service and private news outlets in Germany (analyzed in Lischka 2014a), the general public in Germany (analyzed in Lischka 2015), economic experts in Germany and Switzerland (analyzed in Lischka and Siegert 2013), and companies within the packaged consumer goods industries of food, drinks, tobacco, as well as health and pharmaceutics, and the durable goods industries of textiles and clothing, shoes and leather goods, as well as automobiles in Germany (analyzed in Lischka, Kienzler, and Mellmann 2014). An overview on sources and descriptive of all secondary data used can be found in the Appendix, Table 5.

2 According to the "newspaper" definition of recessions with at least two consecutive quarters of negative GDP growth (Schirwitz 2009), two recessions occur within the observation period. In the 2003/2004 crisis, GDP growth was slightly negative (–0.4%); in the 2008/2009 crisis, the GDP decline was severe (–5.1%) representing the largest GDP decline in Germany's postwar period.

The extent of empirical investigation of the dynamic relations between economic news, economic expectations, and private as well as corporate economic behavior within this book are unique to communication research.

The present book and the related articles (Lischka 2014a; 2015; Lischka, Kienzler, and Mellmann 2014; Lischka and Siegert 2013) apply *n*-th-order multivariate vector autoregression (VAR) models. A VAR model is a system of equations that estimates the *mutual* development of a set of variables over a sample period as a linear function of their past values (Sims 1980). VAR models incorporate the past of one variable to forecast the present of another variable (Y_t, X_t).[3] The VAR models applied have the basic form of

(1a) $\Delta Y_t = \alpha_1 + \beta_{11}\Delta Y_{t-1} + \beta_{12}\Delta Y_{t-2} + \ldots + \beta_{1n}\Delta Y_{t-n} + \lambda_{11}\Delta X_{t-1} + \lambda_{12}\Delta X_{t-2} + \ldots + \lambda_{1n}\Delta X_{t-n} + \varepsilon_{1t}$

(1b) $\Delta X_t = \alpha_2 + \beta_{21}\Delta Y_{t-1} + \beta_{22}\Delta Y_{t-2} + \ldots + \beta_{2n}\Delta Y_{t-n} + \lambda_{21}\Delta X_{t-1} + \lambda_{22}\Delta X_{t-2} + \ldots + \lambda_{2n}\Delta X_{t-n} + \varepsilon_{2t}$

with α being the constant and ε_t being a zero mean white noise process with time-invariant covariance matrix, to measure autoregression (β_1 and λ_2) and short-term impacts (λ_1 and β_2) between the variables of interest and test *directional* Granger causality (Granger 1969).[4] Because VAR models can only be applied to stationary data without time trends (Lutkepohl 2004), non-stationary data are converted into first differences ($Y_t - Y_{t-1}$, Δ), which is a standard procedure to achieve trend stationarity and avoid estimating spurious relations.[5] Hence, VAR models and Granger causality identify a

3 With VAR, contemporaneous and long-term relations are *not* considered.

4 Granger causality tests whether the lags of a variable Y helps to forecast another variable X at time t and therefore goes beyond symmetric, bivariate correlation or covariance. The null hypothesis that X does not Granger cause Y in (1a) is that $\lambda_{11} = \lambda_{12} = \lambda_{1n} = 0$ and that Y does not Granger cause X in (1b) is that $\beta_{21} = \beta_{22} = \beta_{2n} = 0$. The VAR model has already accounted for the effects of past values of Y on Y_t as well as past values of X on X_t (and past values of further variables if included). Dynamic VAR models are therefore a good foundation for testing Granger causality.

5 In time series modeling, it is crucial that the data fulfill the condition of (weak) stationarity to avoid spurious correlations appearing with a low Durbin–Watson *d* statistic revealing autocorrelated residuals, a high R^2, and high significance of the coefficients (Wooldridge 2009; Granger and Newbold 1974). In a strictly stationary time series, all its properties are independent of time. For weak stationarity, mean, variance, and covariance are independent of time (Verbeek 2008, 272). The commonly used augmented Dickey–Fuller (ADF) test is performed to detect the unit roots, and the Kwiatkowski–Phillips–Schmidt–Shin (KPSS) test is used to assess trends and level stationarity for each time series (see e.g., Asteriou and Hall 2011, Chapter 16; Enders 2010, Chapter 4; Scheufele 1999, Chapter VII; Verbeek 2008,

short-term forecasting ability of a *change* in a certain variable to another *beyond* univariate autoregression (β_1 and λ_2) and thus are highly appropriate for the research goal of this study.

This book is structured to theoretically and empirically trace the relations between economic news, economic expectations, and economic behavior. It first defines the theoretical pillars (Chapter 2) and discusses the results of the articles in a broader theoretical context according to the three research questions starting with news making (RQ 1, Chapter 3), followed by the influence of news on economic sentiment (RQ 2, Chapter 4) and the influence of news and economic sentiment on economic behavior (RQ 3, Chapter 5). The present book provides additional analyses, beyond the analyses conducted in the related articles (Lischka 2014a; Lischka, Kienzler, and Mellmann 2014; Lischka and Siegert 2013; Lischka 2015), on the relation between public sentiment and behavior, as well as on the relation between economic news and advertising expenditures (RQ 3, Chapter 5). Chapter 6 provides the overall summary, including an intense discussion of limitations, and conclusions.

Chapter 8). The interested reader can find an illustration of a random walk, unit root and stationary time series reacting to an unexpected shock in Cochrane (2015).

Seasonal components, if detected by testing, are eliminated from the series by including external dummy variables. Due to different seasonal patterns before and after 2001, advertising expenditures are deseasonalised before estimating VAR models. In addition, for advertising expenditures, dotcom outliers are eliminated from the series by including external dummy variables in the specified model to avoid spurious correlations (Kittel and Winner 2005). Therefore, the impacts of advertising expenditures within the VAR models are free from seasonal as well as dotcom crisis effects.

The appropriate lag order of the model is selected by using Akaike's information criterion and Wald lag exclusion statistics. Due to partly relatively short time series, model complexity was kept as low as possible. All VAR models satisfy the Eigenvalue stability condition. As the autocorrelation or a non-white noise process of the residuals ε^ can lead to misinterpretation of the relation between variables, Durbin–Watson test (first-order serial correlation) and a Lagrange-multiplier (LM) test (H0: no autocorrelation at lag order) are performed. The LM test value of the highest lag is reported per VAR model.

All VAR models were estimated using a small-sample degrees-of-freedom adjustment when estimating the error variance-covariance matrix and reports small-sample *t* and *F* statistics (stata.com, 11).The average number of parameters are considered for the small-sample degrees-of-freedom adjustment for the matrix of residuals. For the *F* or *t* distributions, the standard errors from each equation are computed using the degrees of freedom for the equation instead of chi-squared or standard normal distributions.

(These paragraphs originate from Lischka 2015, 383; Lischka, Kienzler, and Mellmann 2014, 37–38, for the most part.)

2 Theoretical considerations

This chapter develops a theoretical model combining real-world economy, economic news and economic sentiment to a triangle of objective, media-based and social realities (2.1), connects the macro to the micro level of the social reality as well as sentiment and behavior to explain collective effects on the macro level (2.2), and traces the temporal relations between the three realities (2.3).

2.1 The triangle of objective, media-based, and social realities

This section traces the relations between the real economy on the level of objective reality, economic news on the level of media reality, and economic expectations and behavior on the level of social reality.

Following Bonfadelli (2004, 237), these relations are illustrated in a triangle of the agenda-setting process as displayed in *Figure 1*.[6] *Figure 1* summarizes the major theoretic approaches, which help to explain the relationships between the three realities, and the data that is typically used to measure each type of reality.

6 Figure 1 is also partly related to Kepplinger's (2007, 17) model of reciprocal effects between media (quality and regional newspapers, TV, radio, internet) and content properties (topics, intensity, tone, frame, consonance) over awareness to reports, cognitions, and emotions of recipients to decisions and consequences. Kepplinger's model is especially relevant to explain media effects on sentiment and behavior of corporate decision makers.

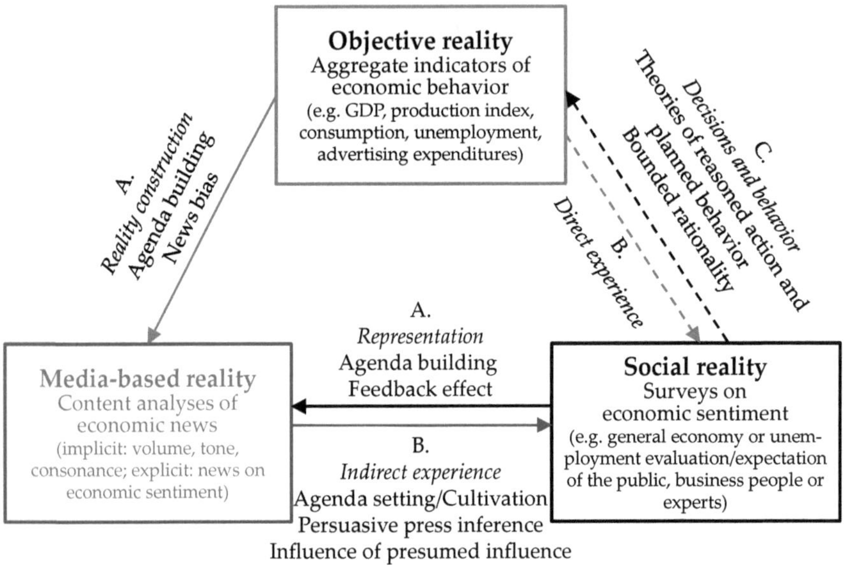

Figure 1: Triangular relations between objective, media-based, and social economic reality

Source: Compiled by the author based on Bonfadelli (2004, 237).

Notes. The media-based reality is usually measured using content analyses, the social reality with surveys, and the objective with real-world indicators. The latter represent aggregate economic behavior of economic agents on a micro level. Indicators of the real economy are categorized in a threefold manner: a) leading indicators that are affected early on, such as economic sentiment or intermediate input goods; b) coincident indicators such as the GDP, industry production or retail sales; c) lagging indicators such as the labor market including employment numbers, wages and salary history as well as inflation and consumer prices (Kater 2008). Indicators of the economic situation in the media-based reality can be implicit—e.g. economic news tone, or explicit—e.g. reports on the development of the GDP. An explicit indicator of the public's economic sentiment is e.g. news reports on the results of surveys on consumer or business sentiment. Consumer or business sentiment are considered to be leading indicators of the state of the economy (e.g., Kater 2008; Levanon 2010; Ludvigson 2004). Indicators of social reality are the evaluations or expectations of different social groups on economic issues. Based on surveys of the public, sentiment indices, such as the University of Michigan's Index of Consumer Sentiment (ICS), become subject to news reporting and are considered leading indicators for the economy (Hagen 2005). Such indices are also computed for business people and economic experts. Hence, social reality measures of economic sentiment should forecast changes in coincident and lagging real-world economic indicators.

For each set of reality dimensions, the relations are theoretically traced in the following.

A. The question whether news can reflect reality has been an issue in news bias studies for decades (see e.g., D'Alessio and Allen 2000; Hackett 1984; Klein and Maccoby 1954; McQuail 1992). Objective reality can *build* the agenda for news, on first or second level (*Reality construction* arrow, *Figure 1*). The concept of media-based reality suggests that the picture of reality offered by media coverage is different from objective reality. Although media reality is regarded as constructed fragment of the objective reality (Kepplinger 2011), it is tied to socially binding models of reality and its social reference mechanisms (Weischenberg 1994). Media reality depends on norms, structures, and actors that are organized on the meso level of the profession's and the media company's formal and informal rules and conventions (Altmeppen 2006, 119). Demers et al. (1989) emphasize that news coverage responds to public concerns such as the unemployment rate and therefore reflects a larger social system. Rössler (1997) acknowledges a feedback effect of the public opinion to the media agenda. This way, consumer sentiment, as one element of social reality, also becomes part of media reality (*Representation* arrow, *Figure 1*). The same is true for business sentiment surveys of the European Commission or the expert economic sentiment of the Ifo institute (Hagen 2005). In addition, such social-reality indicators are regarded to be early indicators of the real-world economic development.

Macro, meso, and micro factors influence news making (Shoemaker and Reese 1996) and the kind of information available in a society. News making (Halloran et al. 1970) is, among many other factors, influenced by news values (Lippmann 1922; Östgaard 1965; Schulz 1976), role conceptions or personal predispositions of a journalist (Weaver et al. 2007), and by commercial motives, ownership, resources or the degree of competition (Beam 2003; Nguyen Vu 2010; Picard 2004; Prat and Strömberg 2012; Russi 2013).[7] The concepts that journalists have of their role range from disseminating information to mobilizing the public, and mainly to interpret reality (Weaver et al. 2007, 146). The

[7] The latter influences on meso and macro level also determine the amount and variety of available information in a society.

degree to which journalists' interpretation substitutes objective reality describes Strömbäck (2008, 240) as phase four of mediatization: "In important respects, the mediated realities replace the notion of a belief in objective realities." Yet interpretation and selection processes can result in biases in news topics, frames, volume, or tone. Hagen (2005) assumes that economic journalists draw conclusions hastily or over-interpret trends. Therefore, economic news is often characterized as negative (see Brettschneider 2003, and Wörsdorfer 2005 for Germany; Lowry 2008 for the USA) and fails to reveal the complexity of the economy (Hagen 2005; Schiffrin 2011a). Depending on the strategic focus and programming mandate, news content differentiates among media (Beam 2003; Nguyen Vu 2010).[8]

The many influences on journalistic reporting suggest shortcomings in how far "the media provide a useful picture of what is 'really' going on" (Funkhouser 1973, 62), especially concerning the economy.

B. An individual's opinion on a certain topic is a result of direct experiences, the experiences of reference groups, interpersonal communication, one's own as well as other people's opinion, and information gathered from the media (see e.g., Ball-Rokeach and DeFleur 1976; Gerbner 1969; McCombs and Shaw 1972; Schenk 1997; Scherer 1990). The model of media dependency (Ball-Rokeach and DeFleur 1976) states that the more important the news is as source of information for the public, the stronger the resulting media effects (*Indirect experience* arrow, *Figure 1*). Conversely, the more direct one's personal experiences on a given topic, the weaker the news influence (*Direct experience* arrow, *Figure 1*).

News media play an important role in the public's agenda (Iyengar and Kinder 1987; McCombs and Shaw 1972; Shaw and

8 This paragraph was part of the author's submission, "How Real is Economic Mass Media Reality? Comparing the Real Economy and Economic News in German News Outlets," to the 2013 Conference of the International Communication Association.

McCombs 1977; Trenaman and McQuail 1961).[9] By paying closer attention to certain topics than to others, news can change the salience[10] of these topics among the public and therefore set the public agenda. In general, the intensity of agenda-setting effects depends on communicator, message, recipient, and environmental or situational variables. The "degree to which the media constitute the most important or dominant source of information" (Shehata and Strömbäck 2011, 234), the need for orientation or familiarity with the topic (Matthes 2006; Wu and Coleman 2009) or the credibility of a news outlet (Wanta and Hu 1994a) affect agenda setting. In addition, when focusing on a certain topic, news defines issues and problems (Noelle-Neumann and Mathes 1987). On a second level of public agenda setting, the attributes of a topic or an object of the media agenda become part of the public agenda. Emphasized attributes are more accessible to the audience than those that are not emphasized. Therefore, news sets *how* the public thinks about certain topics (Ghanem 1997).[11] Providing a macro-level perspective, cultivation theory emphasizes "how the media's institutional practices shaped meanings in the mass production of messages that were then widely disseminated and thereby shaped public knowledge and beliefs over the long term" (Potter 2014, 1017).[12]

9 The media reality potentially *sets* the public agenda serving as an indirect experience. This relation is of major interest for mass communication scholars and many theories and hypotheses were proposed. That media influences what or how people think about certain issues can be explained by first- and second-level agenda setting or the cultivation theory. Mass media effects on recipients can occur on the cognitive, attitudinal, and behavioral level in general. The early "strong effects" paradigm on media effects expected a causal relation between mass media content and mass behavior. Although this paradigm is outdated, a long-term cumulative path from the media agenda to behavior can be drawn employing agenda setting or cultivation. Cultivation theorists as Gerbner 1969 have argued that media coverage is means to reality construction of the public. Further, the public develops beliefs about the beliefs of the public according to Fields and Schuman 1976.

10 As stated by Schenk (1997), public awareness is a result of media use but salience is a result of involvement, interpersonal communication, and individual importance of an issue.

11 This effect is also described with second-order cultivation. According to Hetsroni and Lowenstein(2012, 322), a second-level agenda-setting effect refers to the opinion towards an issue whereas a second-order cultivation effect incorporates resulting sentiment and expectations.

12 According to Potter (2014), agenda-setting theory has shown to have stronger predictive power than cultivation theory in meta analyses.

Comparing effects on the first and second level of agenda setting, Wu and Coleman (2009) show evidence that second-level effects are stronger than first-level effects. For the second level, news objects (e.g. the state of the economy) can be divided into attributes with a substantive dimension, e.g. unemployment, and an affective dimension, e.g. positive, negative or neutral evaluation (Maher 2001; McCombs and Ghanem 2001). The affective dimension incorporates the *tone* of news and ascribes a valence to an attribute that might affect how people think about it. According to Noelle-Neumann and Mathes (1987, 409), the *evaluation* in news reports creates a certain *climate* or *sentiment* of public opinion (see categorization in *Figure* 2). This evaluation can occur through implicit judgments, including frames, or metaphors and explicit judgments of cited actors or journalists in news stories. Hence, news tone and its consonance are related to the second-level of agenda setting, or, creating a climate of opinion through evaluation.

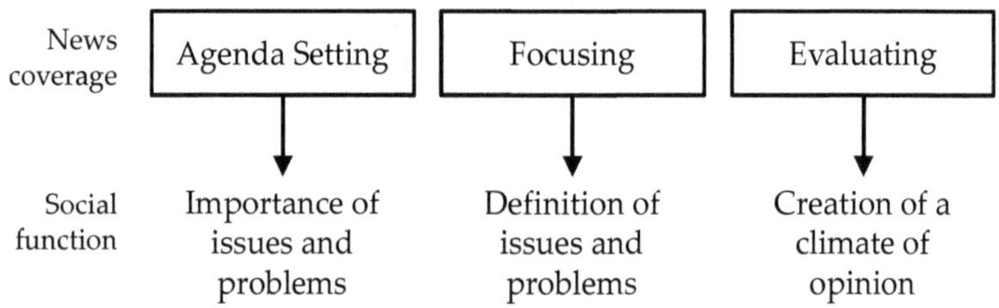

Figure 2: Aspects of reporting and their social function

Source: Noelle-Neumann and Mathes 1987, 409.

Whereas the first- and second-level agenda-setting function states *that* the media agenda and its attributes transfer to the public agenda, this model does not offer a micro-level explanation of *how* and *why* this process occurs. Economic sentiment can develop from experiences people make at their workplaces, hear from friends and family and perceive in their environment, from their attitude towards economic policy decisions, and from economic news. Gunther assumes that

> People may estimate public opinion based on the expressed opinions of friends and acquaintances, or from the speeches of politicians, the actions of prominent people, or published interviews with opinion leaders. They may extrapolate from news of

> demonstrations, strikes or riots, 'man in the street' interviews, or even from letters to the editor. (Gunther 1998, 487)

Therefore, the *slant* of news even only broadly related to a given topic may set a personal opinion and a perceived public opinion whereas both may differentiate from each other (Gunther 1998). Zerback, Koch, and Kramer (2015) demonstrate that explicit cues such as reports on poll results have a strong effect on the perceived climate of opinion but that implicit cues such as arguments guide climate perceptions when explicit cues are absent. They conclude that the slant of an article is used as additional information by recipients to evaluate the climate of opinions when explicit cues are not available, which relates to Noelle-Neumann and Mathes' (1987) evaluation aspect of news (*Figure 2*).

Adoni and Cohen (1978, 62) describe the role of mass media as information source for *economic* sentiment as follows, "In exposing many individuals to simultaneously shared information, mass media might constitute a central tool in fulfilling informational needs and a subjective feeling of understanding, both essential to constructing social reality." Hagen (2005, 294–309) argues that the public opinion on the economy depends on heuristics and the mental organization of economic knowledge. The gratification of orientation through information motivates news reception. News serves as routine environment monitoring, as a basis for economic decision making, and as a cause for interpersonal follow-up communication. Still, for the majority of the public, bounded rationality leads to superficial cognitive processing and deficient representation of economic information (Hagen 2005, 294–309). Because of subjective perception or bounded rationality, the public may use inference heuristics such as the persuasive press inference (Gunther 1998) to form economic expectations based on implicit news cues, "People infer public opinion from their perceptions of the content of media coverage and their assumptions of the persuasive impact of that coverage on others" (Gunther 1998, 486). That is, people also *presume* to know public opinion based on news coverage (Gunther 1998). This may be the case for business people who rely on economic behavior of the public. An observation by Soley and Craig (1992, 7) shows that entrepreneurs assume a connection between economic news and consumer behavior, as an editor reported more than 20 years ago, "...the car dealers (...) want all stories involving auto sales to have a rosy outlook, and they whine about negative economic stories, even if they're on a national level from AP." This example shows that not only the public but also entrepreneurs may "assume that what mass media are saying today must be what the public will be thinking tomorrow" (Gunther 1998, 487) and presume that the public acts according to economic news. This "social construction (...) of audience distortions of reality" (Diefenbach and West 2012, 332) can also be integrated into cultivation theory as the third-person projections affect the beliefs about the behavioral outcomes of others. According to the third-person effect, people overestimate the effect of news on others when they have a manifest or an expert opinion on a certain topic (Perloff 1989) as well as a high self-perceived knowledge on a topic (Rapoport 1982) or perceive a great social distance to a large, heterogeneous group of others (Davison 1983; Perloff 1993; Tewksbury 2002). Therefore, third-person effects, such as the persuasive press influence and the influence of presumed influence, can explain why evaluations or expectations of the behavior of others are biased towards news sentiment (Jensen and Hurley 2005), why own behavior can be affected in turn (Tewksbury, Moy, and Weis 2004), and, overall, why cultivation evolves (Diefenbach and West 2012).

News can be an additional information source that predominantly influences *sociotropic* perceptions (Hagen May 27, 2004; Mutz 1992), i.e., the perception of unemployment or the economy as a social instead of a personal problem. Hence, even when individuals experience unemployment themselves or among family and friends, this issue may be regarded as an important public issue only when it is reported in the news. Only then can the extent of the problem be recognized and expectations for the development of unemployment in a country be developed. As a result, one could argue that economic sentiment depends on the individual media usage. Therefore, scholars referring to a *tight* definition of media effects assume different ways of reporting per media outlet, and analyze effects on an *individual* level using content analysis and panel surveys. Yet news "bring[s] different people and groups together, including people of different levels of formal education and even, to some degree, people with very different annual incomes" (McCombs 1992, 822). Following a *universal* or *broad* approach of media effects, news may lead to an increase in the perceived importance of an issue, which instigates follow-up conversations. Follow-up conversation spreads media content also to non-users of the

media and constitutes a *universal* or *collective media effect*. This assumption neglects effects of different media usage of people and allows for the conducting of analyses on an *aggregate* level.
The collective media effect supposes that the *dominating* media message reaches people directly or indirectly, e.g., through opinion leaders according to the two-step flow of communication (Lazarsfeld, Berelson, and Gaudet 1944; Katz 1957), and people will adapt their opinion and expectations according to it (Maurer 2004, 410). Thus, news consumption as well as personal interactions can cause agenda-setting effects. Indeed, research reveals identical news effects on the agenda of heavy and light media users applying time series analyses (Haller and Norpoth 1997; Krause and Fretwurst 2007; Krause and Gehrau 2007). Haller and Norpoth (1997, 561) report that people not receiving economic news "were by no means making wild guesses about the state of the economy," but were just not as sure as recipients of economic news. Another difference between heavy and light media users is a lower speed of the news effects for light news users (Krause and Fretwurst 2007). This result is in line with the sticky information approach, indicating that the spreading of news is delayed across the public and an updating process on economic issues occurs only every six months or even less often (Easaw and Ghoshray 2010, see also Section 2.3). Thus, changes in the economic expectations of the public occur with a delay.

A powerful influence of collective media effects is the news *consonance* across outlets (Noelle-Neumann 1973; Noelle-Neumann and Mathes 1987). The more consonant media coverage and tone is, the stronger are the media effects on the public (Hagen 2005, 30; Maurer 2004, 410; Peter 2003; 2004). Wanta (1997) argues that similar news agendas across news outlets lead to similar effects on an aggregate level, which is affirmed in Strömbäck and Kiousis' (2010) study. In contrast, if the media coverage is *not* consonant across outlets and people change their opinions according to their media use, *individual-level* analyses show a more accurate picture of media effects than aggregate analyses. Unless media outlets can be differentiated from each other with regard to economic contents or editorial slant (Mast 2012; Spachmann 2005), this study assumes a rather consonant economic news coverage across major news outlets in Germany based on previous research (Degenhard 2011; Eilders 2002; Jarren and Vogel 2009; Noelle-

Neumann and Mathes 1987) and therefore explores news effects on the public as a *collective* effect on an *aggregate* level. Yet differences in economic news per news outlet are investigated. Hence, this study also takes up the question raised by Scheufele (2008) how news effects on a macro level can be theoretically explained and empirically tested.

C. Economic sentiments in turn may guide economic decision making and behavior such as whether to purchase goods, make investments or to save money (*Decisions and behavior* arrow, *Figure 1*).
Attitudes and beliefs affect behavioral intentions and actual behavior according to the theory of reasoned action (Ajzen and Fishbein 1977; 1980; Fazio 1986) and the theory of planned behavior (Ajzen 1991; Ajzen and Fishbein 2005). That is, people act in accordance to their intentions and causal links can be traced from beliefs, attitudes, and intentions to actual performed behavior. According to social psychology, most human behavior is goal-directed and follows more or less elaborate plans as well as behavioral intentions (Ajzen 1985). Behavioral intention, in turn, is guided by attitudes, which can change as a response to novel information. Source, message and recipient factors affect whether information can cause attitudinal change, in a way that "communicator and message variables may influence heuristics (e.g., overheard messages are trustworthy) and message-relevant thoughts (e.g., decisions that the arguments are novel) *within* the recipient" (Johnson, Maio, and Smith-McLallen 2005, 631, italic in original). Thus, message and sources, such as news and news outlets, can determine beliefs, behavioral intentions, and eventually behavior and decisions of recipients.

Rational choice theory claims that decisions are made based on individual preferences in order to maximize benefits. Instead, Herbert A. Simon (1956) argued that agents do not maximize but satisfice needs due to bounded rationality. Internal cognitive constraints, e.g., context dependency of perception and information processing, and environmental constraints, such as the costs of searching for information, lead to biased judgments and decisions. Decision makers may "focus on future experience and (...) ask 'What will I feel then?' rather than 'What do I want now?'" (Tversky and Kahneman 1981, 458). Overly optimistic and overly cautious individuals result at different risk perceptions and decisions (Kahneman and Lovallo 1993). Thus, it has been argued that agents use heuristics for decision making and are rather intuitive than rational (Kahneman 2003; Simon 1987).

In view of bounded rationality, Iyengar and Kinder (1987) as well as Zaller (1992) argue that when making decisions, recipients rely on the topics that are most salient to them due to agenda setting. The salience of beliefs affecting behavioral intentions is also emphasized by Ajzen (1985). Sei-Hill, Scheufele, and Shanahan (2002, 21) stress that the priming process through attribute salience is "a key process for decision making." The model of the influence of presumed influence (Gunther and Storey 2003) proposes that people react according to what they perceive the general public will do. Hence, news may not only affect decisions through forming beliefs about an issue, but also through assumed decisions of others.

Performed behavior also depends on resources and options for a certain kind of behavior (Ajzen 1985). For private consumer behavior, Katona (1957; 1974) stresses that changes in income or savings of an individual affect the purchase of goods. Performed behavior of corporate agents, such as advertising expenditures, also depend on the financial resources of a company (Kienzler and Lischka 2015; Hsu et al. 2002).

The assumptions of bounded rationality and attitude-behavior consistency serve as the micro explanation of why consumer and business sentiment are considered early indicators of the economy. The link between social and objective realities is the behavior of economic actors on a micro level, which in turn adds up to aggregate economic indicators on a macro level. This connection is relevant to explain relations between social and objective reality and is theoretically discussed in the following section.

2.2 The relations between the micro and the macro level

To infer aggregate behavior on a macro level, the micro foundations on an individual level outlined above (C) serve as a powerful explanation. The macro-micro-macro model established by Coleman (1986) or the model of sociological explanation as developed by Esser (1999) offer a theoretical basis for the connection of the macro and the micro level. On a micro level, individual beliefs or sentiments transfer to "orientations to economic behavior" (Coleman 1986, 1322) which is often explained by rational choice theory (Greve, Schnabel, and Schützeichel 2009, 9). Esser (1993) extends this meta theory with concepts of the logic of the situation, selection, and aggregation to explain macro phenomena through the "detour" on individual attitudes and resulting actions on a micro level (Greve, Schnabel, and Schützeichel 2009, 8). Therefore, collectivistic-holistic and individualistic-reductionistic perspectives can be combined and *collective effects* become the central object of explanation which are results of the logic of aggregation (Greve, Schnabel, and Schützeichel 2009, 8). This macro-micro-macro model is illustrated in *Figure 3*. The aggregate level of the objective economic reality at time *t*1 constitutes the context of public beliefs on a micro level transferring to public behavior which in turn aggregates to the objective reality at time *t*2.

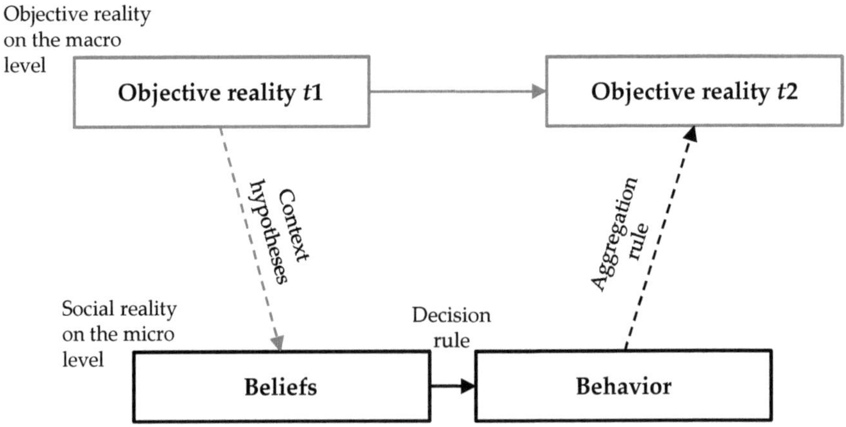

Figure 3: Macro-micro-macro model of collective effects

Source: Compiled by the author based on Greve, Schnabel, and Schützeichel (2009, 8).

According to Coleman (1990, 198), there are three general properties in collective behavior.

1. "They involve a number of people carrying out the same or similar actions at the same time."

2. "The behavior exhibited is transient or continually changing, not in an equilibrium state," which is a requirement for the detection of changes on an aggregate macro level.
3. "There is some kind of dependency among the actions; individuals are not acting independently," for which media plays a decisive role.

Coleman (1990) uses bank and stock market panics as an example of collective behavior. The economic behavior of private individuals may not entirely fit the definition of collective behavior since people may act independently due to their individual income expectations (Katona 1974; 1975). Their actions may not directly affect others' actions and vice versa. Yet to assess whether it is a good moment to make major purchases it may be rational to *orient oneself* towards the opinion and actions of other members of society especially when the economic situation is insecure. Therefore, major purchase decisions have single- and may acquire double-contingency characteristics.[13] Robert J. Shiller (2005, 85) argues in his book *Irrational Exuberance* that "...significant market events generally occur only if there is similar thinking among large groups of people, and the news media are essential vehicles for the spread of ideas." Hence, when actors' beliefs become similar, for example through news reports, their behavior will be alike and changes in aggregate market results such as private consumption or investor behavior should be visible. For example, sunspots deriving from self-fulfilling prophecies or herding behavior may lead to similar economic behavior.[14]

A *corporate* agent acts purposefully, considering the interests of the multiple principals and agents of the company (Coleman 1990). One area of corporate decision making are advertising activities. Seeing advertising

13 Coleman (1990, 902) describes single-contingency collective behavior as having, "a feedback loop from the actor's current action through its consequences to the actor's future actions. He uses information about others' previous actions to better predict those consequences." In case of double-contingency collective behavior, "the feedback loop contains the strategic actions of others. The actor acts; his action affects others, who act in such a way as to influence his future actions in a way that will be beneficial to them. Recognizing this, he in turn acts in such a way that their actions will be beneficial to him." These presumptions on the behavior of others can be applied to public and also to corporate economic behavior and relates to third-person effects described in section B.

14 Harrison and Weder (2006) argue that sunspots caused and can explain the entire depression era in the USA from 1929 to 1938.

budgeting decisions from a macro-micro-macro model of collective effects, advertising budgeting depends on the beliefs that the decision is based on. A crucial belief are sales expectations (Kienzler and Lischka 2015; Lischka, Kienzler, and Mellmann 2014) which in turn may also depend on the perception of public economic sentiment—or, as suggested by the persuasive press inference, on business news. Therefore, corporate actors will also consider their customers' (assumed) behavior when taking action.

Relating to Coleman's second property mentioned above, an aggregation may conceal inter-individual or -company differences in private or corporate economic behavior. Scheufele (2008) lines out the dilemma when aggregating using the example of lay and professional investor behavior in stock markets. He points out that the role of media and the social environment as well as the readiness to assume risk differ on the micro level. When using secondary data on the aggregate level, these micro differences and social dynamics are not evident anymore. On the other hand, changes in behavior that is caused by media coverage is only relevant *when* there are visible changes on the macro level (Scheufele 2008, 349). Hence, even when inter-individual and -corporate differences remain hidden on a macro level, the collective behavior potentially features the three properties outlined by Coleman (1990, 198).

Figure 4 proposes an overall model connecting objective, media-based, and social realities differentiating into the macro and the micro level. Media-based reality is connected to objective reality and constitutes part of the context actors perceive beside objective reality. Objective and media-based media realities influence actors' beliefs. Rational choice, bounded rationality, and the theories of reasoned action and planned behavior explain the decision rule on which behavior is based on. Individual behavior aggregates to objective reality at time *t*2. That is, private purchases add up to industry sales as well as national private consumption and become part of the GDP. Corporate advertising expenditures add up to industry and national advertising expenditures. Media reality can also report on the beliefs and behavior of actors at *t*1 and *t*2.

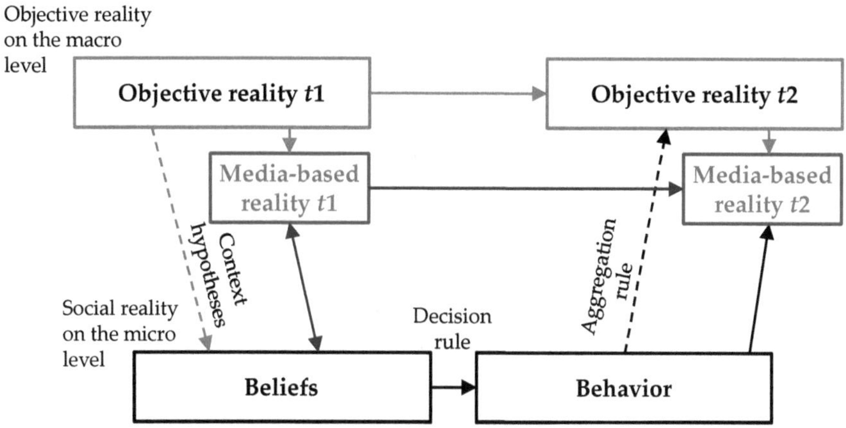

Figure 4: Macro-micro-macro model of collective effects including the media-based reality

Source: Compiled by the author based on Greve, Schnabel, and Schützeichel (2009, 8).

2.3 Temporal relations between objective, media-based, and social realities

Temporal relations between the different realities in *Figure 1* can be assumed as shown in *Figure 4*. Rössler (1997, 103) suggests that media affect public opinion at time *t*1 and *t*2 as well as vice versa, media coverage follows its own trend, and so does the public agenda. *Figure 5* considers the temporal course among objective, media-based, and social realities. First, all realities depend on their own past (autoregression).[15] Second, the triangular relations remain as indicated in *Figure 1*. But these relations may

15 In an autoregressive (AR) process, the current value at time *t*1 is a linear result of its past values. The development of the objective, media-based, and social realities cannot be considered random white noise processes that do not depend on their own past at all but naturally at least somewhat depend on their own past. Although news deal with new events, news events have a history and may be trending topics as argued by Hagen (2005, 141). Often, a time series (Y) consists of stochastic trend (β) or deterministic time trend (αt), a drift (μ), a stationary component, and noise (u) in the form of $Y_t = \mu + \alpha t + \beta Y_{t\text{-}1} + u_t$ (Enders 2010, 181–86; Verbeek 2008, 284). Lischka and Seufert (2015) explain that most time series data are some kind of AR process in greater detail.

occur instantaneously at $t1$ or $t2$ as well as, over time, between $t1$ and $t2$, and so on.

In the resulting model (*Figure 5*), the objective reality at $t2$ depends on its own past and the past of the social reality, since the social reality leads to economic behavior, which eventually accumulates to indicators of the objective reality.

The media-based reality at $t2$ depends on its own past, the past and present objective reality, and the past and present social reality. News may report about the past social reality when reporting about consumer or business climate survey results. Although the present social economic reality may not be fully directly observable, news can report about statements revealing contemporary opinions of experts or consumers. Assuming that indicators of the current objective economic situation may be perceivable in the people's daily lives, such as the bustle on shopping streets or the construction activity in a city can influence economic sentiment as discussed in Lischka (2015), the present objective reality may also become part of the news.

The social reality depends on its own past, the past and present of the objective as well as the media reality. The speed of the media agenda diffusion and the quality of direct experiences with the objective reality influence the stickiness of the social reality at time t.

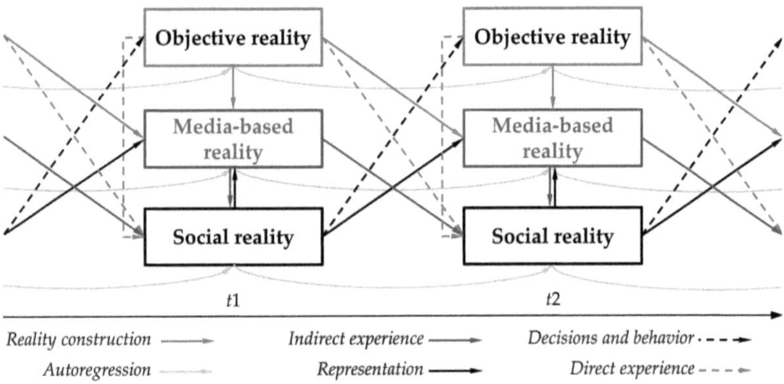

Figure 5: Temporal relations between objective, media-based, and social realities

Source: Compiled by the author based on Rössler (1997, 108).
Note. Captions relate to arrows in *Figure 1*.

Concerning the stickiness of social reality, Katona states the following.

> Social learning, that is, the acquisition of new opinions and attitudes by very many people, is slow and gradual, except under the influence of major events which call for a reorganization of the cognitive map and which occur rarely (for example, outbreak of war, revolution, runaway inflation). (Katona 1968, 22)

Previous research suggests that economic news spreads unevenly and slowly through a population, as studies on news diffusion (Greenberg 1964; Nguyen Vu and Gehrau 2010; Valente 1993; Winter and Eyal 1981; Stone and McCombs 1981) or stickiness of information diffusion show (Döpke et al. 2008; Carroll 2003; Easaw and Ghoshray 2010).

The time lag from *t*1 to *t*2 in agenda setting is said to lie within one week and several months, depending on the publishing frequency and reach of a news outlet type as well as the public interest in a topic and the news salience (Stone and McCombs 1981; Wanta and Hu 1994b; Winter and Eyal 1981). Based on the media agenda of two national news magazines in the U.S., Stone and McCombs (1981) show that the public first registers an average topic after two to six months. Winter and Eyal (1981) conclude that a time span of four to six weeks is optimal for detecting agenda-setting effects. TV news are found to have the shortest agenda-setting effect time lag with one to three weeks, followed by daily newspapers with three to five weeks and magazines with eight to eleven weeks according to Wanta and Hu (1994b).

Concerning *economic* sentiment, Easaw and Ghoshray (2010) reveal that U.S. households update their expectations of the aggregate economy in twelve and 18 months in response to bad and good news, respectively. Similarly, Doms and Morin (2004) show that the updating process is faster during recessions. An update of employment expectations takes between two to five months in high and low news states, respectively, which are associated with recession and non-recession times, respectively (Doms and Morin 2004).

Consequently, the relations between objective, media-based and social realities need to be analyzed over time allowing for a lagged influence of the objective and media-related realities on the social reality of up to 18 months,[16] depending on the overall economic situation, and ideally with a weekly or monthly data frequency from *t*1 to *t*2.

16 As stated in Footnote 5, the eventual appropriate lag order of the VAR models estimated in the present book was selected by using Akaike's information criterion (AIC) and Wald lag exclusion statistics, which are post-hoc tests of a VAR estimation. AIC measures the model quality based on the given data, which is used to compare different VAR models, and Wald tests whether the coefficients of the endogenous variables at a given lag are jointly zero and thus irrelevant for the VAR estimation. Most often, it was statistically sufficient to include up to three lags, i.e., three past months, in the VAR models of the present study.

3 Economic news and the real economy

This chapter answers the first research question, *How closely is economic news related to the real-world economy?* A series of influences at the macro level of the environment, at the meso level of the media organization, and at the micro level of the individual journalist are responsible for differences between news and reality. To approach the answer, first, the micro level of journalists' ability to depict the real world is observed (3.1); second, the influence of their working environment on journalistic output is discussed (3.2); and third, the relation between economic news and economic indicators is estimated (3.3).

3.1 The ability of journalists to report on the real economy

This section explores whether economic journalists expect themselves to report in an unbiased way on the objective economic reality. Furthermore, it discusses the news prominence of a weak economy in times of the recession connected to the financial crisis.

The book *Bad news: How America's business press missed the story of the century* edited by Anya Schiffrin (2011a) describes the role of the business press in the financial crisis and cites the U.S.-American television host and satirist Jon Stewart who criticizes financial news as naïve in view of the crisis as follows.

> "There are three twenty-four-hour financial networks. All their slogans are like, 'We know what's going on on Wall Street.' But then you turn it on during the crisis, and they're like, 'We don't know what's going on.' It'd be like turning on the Weather Channel in a hurricane and they're just doing this: [shuddering] 'Why am I wet?! What's happening to me? And it's so windy!'" (Schiffrin 2011a, book jacket)

Especially in the course of the financial crisis, economic or financial journalism was criticized to be unable to identify and forecast this major event.

Also before the financial crisis, economic news was criticized to not effectively report on the economy, not report in an unbiased way, as well as not following the tradition of investigative journalism (Doyle 2006; Manning 2013; Marron et al. 2010; Mast 2012, 66–68; Robertson 2010; Schiffrin 2011b; Schifferes 2011). Some time ago, Singletary et al. complained about news reporting related to economic forecasts.

> In fact, given the precarious nature of forecast journalism compared to conventional reporting of elapsed events, one might consider the performance of 'Periscope' and 'Washington Whispers' acceptable if not commendable. (Singletary et al. 1983, 344)

Generally, intrinsic, i.e., event-internal, and extrinsic news factors, i.e., organizational and procedural constraints or journalists' attitudes, are said to drive journalistic selection and determine what is reported about the economy (Hagen 2005; Hanitzsch and Mellado 2011). Hagen (2005, 78, 181) assumes that economic and business journalists might hastily draw conclusions or over-interpret economic trends. A common complaint in research has been for some time that economic news overemphasize negative economic developments (e.g., Brettschneider 2003; Harrington 1989; Soroka 2006). Whereas, on the contrary, an alarming news language during a crisis is needed to describe the nature of the event (Schifferes and Coulter 2013).[17] These inabilities to report about the real-world economy raise the question whether economic news fails its critical role as guardian of democratic societies (Schiffrin 2011a).

Journalists are aware of their inability to provide a reproduction of the real world (Weischenberg 1994, 427). Although German business journalists describe their most important merit with providing *neutral* and *precise* information for the audience (Mast 2012, 146), the complexity of economic relations, the lack of a watchdog role among economic journalists,[18] and insufficient skills are found to have collectively inhibited the

17 Interestingly, media users seem to appreciate negative economic news since they feel better informed about economic developments when news have a negativity bias as reported by van Dalen et al. (05.02.2015).

18 About 60% of German business journalists want to offer support for the life of their audience suggesting a service or news-you-can-use role of journalism (Spachmann 2005, 321).

forecasting of the financial crisis. A German financial journalist at the former *Financial Times Deutschland* describes an enhancement in his watchdog behavior after the financial crisis.

> "Even as an economic journalist I didn't try so hard to understand it because I thought there were other journalists at *Financial Times Deutschland* who were experts on this subject who understood this better. But after the Lehman's crash my approach changed totally. I wanted to understand more, I attended more conferences, spoke to more people. I am definitely more conscious of the whole subject." (Picard, Selva, and Bironzo 2014, 15, italic in original)

The cross-national Worlds of Journalism Study collects evaluations from newspaper, magazine, TV, radio, and news agency journalists in 21 countries on attitudes towards the journalistic standard of unbiased reporting among other topics. Especially the attitudes towards the items "I do not allow my own beliefs and convictions to influence my reporting," "I remain strictly impartial in my work," and "I think that journalists can depict reality as it is," measured on a 5-point scale from strongly agree (1) to strongly disagree (5) give an idea of journalists' stand on unbiased news coverage (Worlds of Journalism Study 2007). Table 1 reveals results for journalists usually working on no specific beat or in a non-economy related beat (n = 282) versus journalists usually working on an economic, business, or financial beat (n = 18) from the USA, Germany and Switzerland. The economic journalists (n = 18) predominantly work for newspapers or online news outlets. The fieldwork was conducted between August and October in 2007 and thus took place before the collapse of major financial institutes indicating the start of the financial crisis in 2008 but during the U.S. subprime mortgage crisis in 2007, which is regarded as catalyst for the financial crisis (Beck and Wienert 2009).

Results are reported in Table 1 for the three selected countries together, and broken down by journalists working on non-economic beats and those working on economic beats for all three countries and per country. Overall, journalists in all fields agree that their own beliefs do not influence their reporting, that their work is impartial. However, journalists in all three countries are on average undecided as to whether their work depicts reality as it is. Journalists working on an economic beat agree less strongly on all three items, with a significant ($p < .05$) difference for the influence of their own beliefs that is especially strong in Switzerland and the USA. German and Swiss economic journalists doubt that they depict reality as it is or are undecided about it, whereas their US colleagues tend to agree that they correctly depict reality. German economic journalists in this sample have strong doubts as to whether they produce economic news that reflects the real world correctly. Swiss economic journalists are less persuaded than their colleagues on other beats or with no specific beat that their own beliefs do not have an influence on their reporting. The results for economic journalists are based on a few cases only and have to be interpreted with caution. However, overall, journalists are not convinced that they can depict reality as it is—and economic journalists in Germany doubt this most strongly.

Table 1: Evaluations of reporting standards of journalists working on non-economic and economic beats in Germany, Switzerland, and the United States

		Total	Non-economy	Economy	D		CH		USA	
Items		D+CH+USA	D+CH+USA	D+CH+USA	Non-economy	Economy	Non-economy	Economy	Non-economy	Economy
No influence	Mean	1.95	1.92_a	2.44_b	1.99_a	2.14_a	1.91_a	2.83_b	1.86_a	2.40_a
on reporting	(Stdev.)	(0.95)	(.91)	(1.38)	(0.90)	(1.07)	(0.83)	(1.60)	(0.99)	(1.67)
Remain strictly	Mean	2.1	2.09_a	2.29_a	2.08_a	2.14_a	2.21_a	2.67_a	1.98_a	2.00_a
impartial	(Stdev.)	(0.97)	(0.96)	(1.26)	(0.89)	(1.35)	(0.93)	(1.51)	(1.04)	(0.82)
Depict reality	Mean	2.58	2.55_a	3.00_a	2.87_a	3.86_b	2.61_a	3.00_a	2.18_a	1.80_a
as it is	(Stdev.)	(1.27)	(1.25)	(1.57)	(1.24)	(1.21)	(1.27)	(1.90)	(1.14)	(0.84)
Number of cases		300	282	18	93	7	94	6	95	5

Notes. 5-point Likert scale from strongly agree (1) to strongly disagree (5), subscript $_b$ indicates a significant difference to mean with subscript $_a$ within one group at $p < .05$ (two-sided *t*-test, Bonferroni corrected). Non-economy: journalists working on no specific beat or on a non-economy related beat, Economy: journalists working on an economic, business, or financial beat. Data source: The Worlds of Journalism Study; fieldwork August through October 2007.

Hence, the economic and business journalists surveyed do not expect to be able to copy economic reality in news reports. The reasons for which journalists doubt that there is no influence on reporting can also be found on the organizational level of the news outlet. The next section will discuss organizational influences on journalistic work to report on the economy.

3.2 Organizational influences on reporting

Besides constraints at the micro level, constraints at the macro level of the environment and the meso level of the organization are responsible for differences between the news reported by different news outlets. In this context, Spachmann (2005) reveals clearly differentiated news topic patterns and Mast (2012) affirms different editorial strategies across German economic print outlets. Depending on the degree of market orientation and strategic focus, content differentiates among media (Beam 2003). Russi (2013) shows that product differentiation through news content depends on available resources and concludes that competition and resources are crucial determinants of strategic product differentiation. According to Prat and Strömberg (2012, 168), competition may increase news bias and "force newspapers to slant their news in order to avoid price competition," which makes news less informative. Picard (2004, 57) states that "The primary content of newspapers today is commercialized news and features designed to appeal to broad audiences, to entertain, to be cost effective and to maintain readers whose attention can be sold to advertisers." Economic pressure and commercial ownership are found to have a negative influence on the quantity and diversity of foreign TV news (Nguyen Vu 2010). Thus, commercial motives, the existence of a programming mandate and related income sources may alter news content across private and public-service outlets, as argued in Lischka (2014a).

Shoemaker and Reese (1996) assume that the organization has more influence on news than an individual journalist. Potter (2014, 1031) argues from a cultivation-theory stance that institutional practices shape media content. Based on the Worlds of Journalism Study, Hanitzsch et al. (2010) reveal a hierarchical structure from stronger meso- to weaker macro-level influences on journalists' work. The immediate environment of the journalist—i.e., professional, procedural, and organizational aspects—is the most powerful influence on the day-to-day work of journalists, and reference groups, economic and politics are less powerful influences. For German and Swiss journalists as well as those in other countries, Hanitzsch and Mellado (2011) confirm this hierarchy.

Furthermore, Schiffrin (2011b, 1) relates the failures of news reporting during the financial crisis also to the economic situation of media organizations suffering from decreasing advertising income, which led to staff layoffs and eventually to shut downs of business news outlets, "Beset by job losses and the migration of advertising revenue to the Internet, traditional media was in a decline that seemed irreversible." Economic problems increased pressure and thus the likability of reporting failures on a micro level of the journalist, "Afraid of their jobs and struggling with the most complicated story that many of them had ever covered—all the while worrying about their own futures" (Schiffrin 2011b, 2). Thus, the macro level of the economy affects the news organization's financial situation at the meso level, in turn the journalists at the micro level, and eventually their reporting. This economic context and financing situation of news media organizations provides additional relevance for studying influences of corporate advertising expenditures (see Section 5.2).

Based on the model of sociological explanation (Esser 1999), Reinemann (2007) and Jäckel (2007) propose a structural-individualistic model incorporating the macro level situation, its impact on the situation and action of the media organization at a meso level, and in turn its impact on the situation and action of the journalist on a micro level in order to explain e.g. the degree of tabloidization in news. Based on this model, illustrated in *Figure 6*, a collective news bias on aggregate level can be explained by actions of media companies and journalists. Vice versa, journalists' internal conditions, the micro level, are directly linked to journalistic action, i.e., news production. These internal conditions are influenced by the media organization forming the journalists' external condition. This meso level of the organization is influenced by its external conditions on the environmental, macro level. According to Hanitzsch et al. (2010), the closer a level is to journalistic action, the greater is the perceived influence by journalists.

Lischka (2014a) investigates the influence of revenue incentives indicated by the dual media system in Germany on news characteristics. Different revenue incentives between public-service and private news outlets alter the need to fit news to demands of mainstream audiences, which was previously argued by Hamilton (2004). Whereas privately advertising-funded news outlets have to sell profitable audiences to advertisers, public-service outlets depend on license fees and follow a programming mandate.[19] This macro-level context shapes the situation of the media company

19 Yet also public-service news outlets have to adapt to demands of mainstream audiences in order to retain legitimacy, ascribed by stakeholder groups, and their "right to exist". Public-service TV channels also depend "highly on the market environment they operate in and on the extent of their dependency on advertising revenues" (Nguyen Vu 2010, 192).

and its action (see *Figure 6*). This in turn shapes the situation of the journalists and their action resulting in output differences. Hence, Reinemann's (2007) and Jäckel's (2007) models serve as a micro foundation for the argumentation that revenue incentives lead to differences in news.

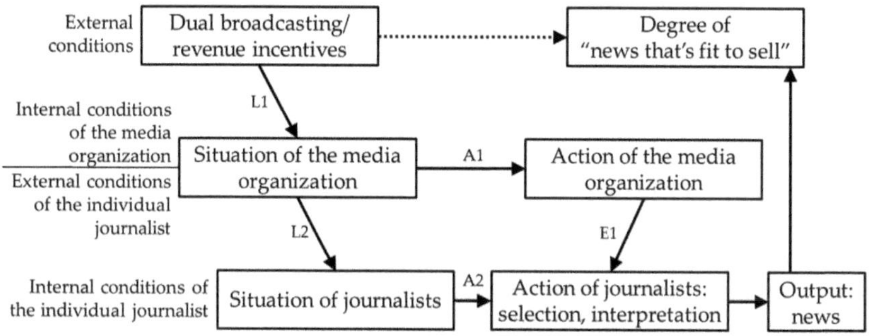

Figure 6: Action-related model of the sociological explanation relating revenue incentives and journalists' selection and interpretation processes

Source: Compiled by the author based on Reinemann (2007, 55, 62) and Jäckel (2007, 91).

Notes. L1, 2: logic of the situation, macro-micro transition: linking rules that determine relevant aspects of the situation, evaluations, and expectations; A1, 2: logic of selection, micro-micro/meso-meso transition: application of an expectancy-value formulation to evaluate and select action alternatives; E1: logic of aggregation, micro-macro transition: aggregation rules to explain collective effects, downwards arrow in Reinemann (2007, 62).

Hence, environmental and organizational circumstances affect journalists' work and therefore shape journalistic output. Considering organizational as well as environmental influences on journalists, it seems to be impossible to produce unbiased economic news. The following section will investigate the relation between economic news and economic indicators.

3.3 The relation between economic news and economic indicators

This section describes the characteristics of economic news and agenda building referring to results of Lischka (2014a), Lischka and Siegert (2013) and Lischka (2015). Lischka (2014a) compares the economic news development in four major German news outlets from 2002 to 2010 including the period of the global financial crisis. Lischka and Siegert (2013) include economic news of the major Swiss public-service news outlet from 2007 to 2011. Lischka (2015) investigates how strongly economic news is derived from the real-world economy or from public expectations.

Hagen (2005, 86) claims that economic journalists have to rely on economic statistics for their reporting. This implies a close relationship between real-world economic indicators and economic news. A study by Hollanders and Vliegenthart (2011) supports this assumption demonstrating a forecasting ability of stock market indices for news. Doms and Morin (2004) reveal periods lacking a consistency between economic indicators and economic news. In addition, Goidel et al. (2010) reveal media type differences in the correlation between real-world economic indicators and news. In their study, national print news (*New York Times*) and local broadcast news were in alignment with economic indicators, whereas local print news and national broadcast news (*CBS Evening News*) were not. In contrast, the national print and broadcast news were in alignment with state unemployment numbers whereas local news were not. The latter result can be explained by the regional focus of news outlets. The former may be connected with a comparably moderate number of negative reporting by national print and local broadcast news, whereas *CBS News* and local print had highest and lowest numbers of negative reports.

Unexpected events can unhinge news routines. Scheufele (2003, 104) argues that reporting processes and therefore content change corresponding to the novelty of a situation. As a result of a crucial event, such as an unexpected economic crisis as the financial crisis following the subprime crisis in 2007, and a shortage of information, editorial work processes change from a *routine* to an *orientation* mode. During this orientation period, journalists realign the criteria of news production and new frames of reference can be developed. Schifferes and Coulter (2013, 240) report for the *BBC News* website that economic news sentiment at the beginning of the crisis in September 2008 was about equally positively and negatively and turned uniformly negatively after three weeks when "the market contagion began to impact the real economy," which can be regarded as indicating an orientation mode period. Blondheim, Segev, and Cabrera (2015) apply time-lag analysis to online economic news of the ten major Internet languages during the economic crisis period from 2009 to 2012. Their results reveal, unsurprisingly, that negative GDP growth leads to higher salience in reporting in GDP for major and small economies. In addition, after the onset of the Euro crisis in 2009, economic news was much richer in reporting cross-country and global relations of economies. Likewise, Kleinnijenhuis, Schultz, and Oegema (2015) show an increased frame complexity in economic news during the years of the financial crisis (from 2007 to 2012) in articles of US, UK, and German newspapers. Hence, an orientation mode period may have changed economic reporting.

During the financial crisis period, Lischka (2014a) shows that the volume of economic news on German TV news increases greatly between 2007 and 2010, especially on public-service channels, whereas the volume of economic news decreases in a tabloid newspaper from 2007 onward. The Swiss public-service news show reports less often on the economy and does not increase its news volume until 2010 (Lischka and Siegert 2013, 177, Figure 1). Between 2002 and 2006, the news topic categories[20] of state-context-location, employment, and the general economy are the top-three economic topics for all four news outlets. From 2007 to 2010, the topic of the general economy becomes the number-two news topic. Also in Swiss public-service news, the topic of state-context-location is often the most important. However, Swiss economic news reports more often on other economic topics (Lischka and Siegert 2013, 178, Table 1), such as news on individual businesses or industries (Sommer et al. 2010). On average, news tone is negative to neutral between 2002 and 2005 for all outlets and increases in 2006/7 to neutral. After 2007 the news tone of the TV news shows degenerates. Yet public-service news tone degenerates more strongly than the news tone of the private TV news show. The news tone of the tabloid newspaper does not decline compared to its average in 2006. Hence, the

20 Economic news topics used in the present study comprise the categories (1) state-context-location (economic policy, national debt, laws, orders, bureaucracy, general ability to compete, employment protection, environmental specifications, protection against dismissal, business tax, income tax, value added tax, subsidies, tariff policy, infrastructure, foreign direct investments), (2) the general economy, (3) employment, (4) consumer and business sentiment, (5) productivity and labor costs, (6) prices and inflation, (7) currency, (8) external trade, (9) GNP and GDP, (10) order entries, (11) income, and (12) minor topics (bankruptcies, startups, investments, innovations). Since there is a strong political dimension to economic reporting (Doyle 2006, 444) and politics and the economy are interwoven, especially during the financial crisis when many governmental interventions were made (Quiring and Weber 2012; Sommer 2013), it is necessary to include economic–political news.

negative consequences of the financial crisis were reflected in TV news. But journalistic interpretation processes differ according to media category and revenue model. In Switzerland, public-service news tone does not degenerate until 2009 and reveals a more volatile picture than German public-service news (Lischka and Siegert 2013, 177, Figure 2).

Lischka (2015) estimates as to whether changes in real-world economic figures forecast changes in news tone (*NT*, coded positive (1), neutral (0) or negative (−1)), consonance (*NC*, inverted standard deviation of news tone), or volume (*NV*, absolute numbers of reports or articles) for the general situation of the economy and employment. News of the major German news outlets with the highest reach are used: the TV news shows *ARD Tagesschau, ZDF heute, RTL aktuell,* and the tabloid newspaper *BILD*. The news outlet with the largest audience in terms of reach (9.62 million and 9.14 million viewers in 2002 and 2011, respectively) is the major evening news show *ARD Tagesschau,* a public service broadcast, followed by the major evening news show *ZDF heute* (5.17 million and 3.97 million viewers in 2002 and 2010, respectively), the second public service broadcast in Germany, a major commercial broadcaster's evening news, *RTL aktuell* (3.89 million and 3.91 million viewers in 2002 and 2010, respectively) (Zubayr and Gerhard 2005; 2012). The fourth most important news outlet in terms of circulation is the commercial daily tabloid, *BILD,* whose circulation is in decline (4.05 million and 2.94 million in 2002 and 2010, respectively) (IVW 2013). The selection of news outlets and the data measurement are based upon detecting collective media effects, which are explained in Lischka (2015, 382–85), representing Germany's pluralistic media structure.
Figure 7 displays the z-standardized data[21] for news on the general economy[22] and the production index. Throughout the observation period, news

21 Observations are z-transformed by subtracting the mean and dividing by the standard deviation. Thus, all data are displayed on one scale that indicates the standard score, i.e., the number of standard deviations of which the data are above or below the mean, which is set to zero (0). The original means are reported in the Appendix, Table 5.

22 The news content data for the observation period from January 2002 to June 2011 (n = 114 months) are kindly provided by the research company Media Tenor. The unit of analysis is each print article and TV report on economic topics referring to Germany on TV news shows and in the first three pages of the selected newspaper (*BILD*), as it does not hold a separate business news section. Except for the weather forecast, TV news shows are coded in their entirety. Qualifying criteria for further coding of articles and reports were economic topics, recent German domestic politics, German foreign affairs, and reports on the

and the production index develop quite similarly by trend. However, news tone, consonance and volume develop in a more volatile way from one month to the next. During the recession period, news tone starts degenerating earlier than the production index. News volume and consonance increase during the 2008/9 recession. After the end of the recession, the trends develop similarly again. Interestingly, news consonance is high during downturns and lower during upturns. News volume becomes more volatile in the second half of 2007 and shows a strong increase of nearly up to four standard deviations towards the end of the 2008/9 recession period.

Figure 8 displays the z-standardized data for news on employment[23] and the unemployment rate. News tone develops contrary to the unemployment rate revealing a more negative and more consonant news tone when unemployment increases. Again, news consonance increases when unemployment is higher and declines with lower unemployment, revealing higher consonance when news tone is negative. Also for this topic, news tone, consonance, and volume develop in a more volatile way than the unemployment rate. News volume shows two peaks in the middle of 2004 and 2005 when unemployment increases. In 2007 and 2008, unemployment numbers and employment news volume decrease. Between 2010 and 2011, news volume increases while unemployment continues to decline. The trends of news and economic indicators for the general economy and unemployment develop at least to some degree in alignment. News tone and consonance on the general economy seems to be early, indicating the decline of the economic situation at the end of 2008.

European Union or its institutions. The numbers of coded economic news stories are 7,289 (*ARD Tagesschau*), 7,311 (*ZDF heute*), 4,559 (*RTL Aktuell*), and 7,308 (*BILD*) summing up to a total of 26,467. The analysis of the current section selects all reports and articles on the *general economy*, i.e., dealing with the topics of national income, gross national product (GNP), GDP, the general economic situation, and economic growth for news on the general economic situation (N = 4,152). Total observations on news on the general economy amount to 1,095 for *ARD Tagesschau*; 1,267 for *ZDF heute*; 711 for *RTL aktuell*; and 1,079 for *BILD* (Lischka 2015, 379).

23 *Employment* news comprises all reports and articles on employment, unemployment, occupation, apprenticeships, labor force participation rate, the professional education system, and the professional qualification of the population (N = 4,806). Total observations on the employment amount to 1,148 for *ARD Tagesschau*; 1,100 for *ZDF heute*; 996 for *RTL aktuell*; and 1,562 for *BILD* (Lischka 2015, 379).

The dynamic relations between real-world economic indicators and corresponding news are tested with VAR models in Lischka (2015). Results (Lischka 2015, 384, Table 1) as illustrated in *Figure 9* reveal that it is primarily *news interpretation,* measured with economic news tone and consonance, that is set by changes in economic indicators confirming previous research (Behr and Iyengar 1985; Hagen 2005, 154, 171; Wu et al. 2002; Blondheim, Segev, and Cabrera 2015). However, weaker relationships between the real-world economic indicator production index and news tone are found with news on the general economy, whereas the news tone of employment news depends greatly on changes in the unemployment rate. News tone on the general economy depends greatly on the news tone of the previous month. Once an interpretation on the general economy is established, this is stable for two months. News interpretation is more consistent when the economy deteriorates or unemployment increases and is less consistent when the economy and unemployment improve—which may be caused by asymmetric responses by journalists to negative events (Soroka 2006; Wu et al. 2002).

News selection measured with news volume cannot be forecast by economic indicators for both news topics. The volume of news on the general economy depends greatly on its own past. During the 2008/9 recession, the more pessimistic public expectations Granger cause an increase in news volume on the general economy. This relationship can be interpreted as news supply on the topic complying with the public demand. In contrast, employment news volume decreases as volume on news on the general economy increases, revealing a volume adjustment due to changes in the news agenda or to shortage of space and time.

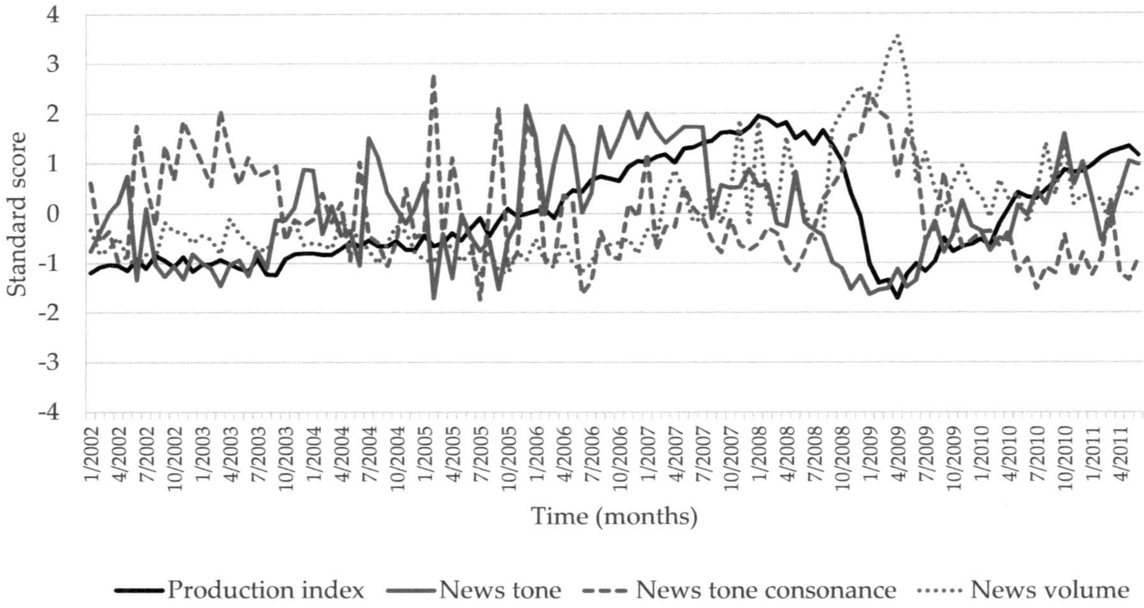

Figure 7: The production index and news on the general economy

Notes. Observation period Jan 2002 – Jun 2011. All data are z-transformed. The recession periods comprise Q1 2003 to Q3 2004 and Q2 2008 to Q1 2009. News tone, consonance and volume are monthly means and sums respectively of the total news on the general economy of four news outlets: *ARD Tagesschau*, *ZDF heute*, *RTL aktuell*, *BILD* (Lischka 2015, 382–85). The German production index is published by the German Federal Statistical Office and is adjusted for working day and season.

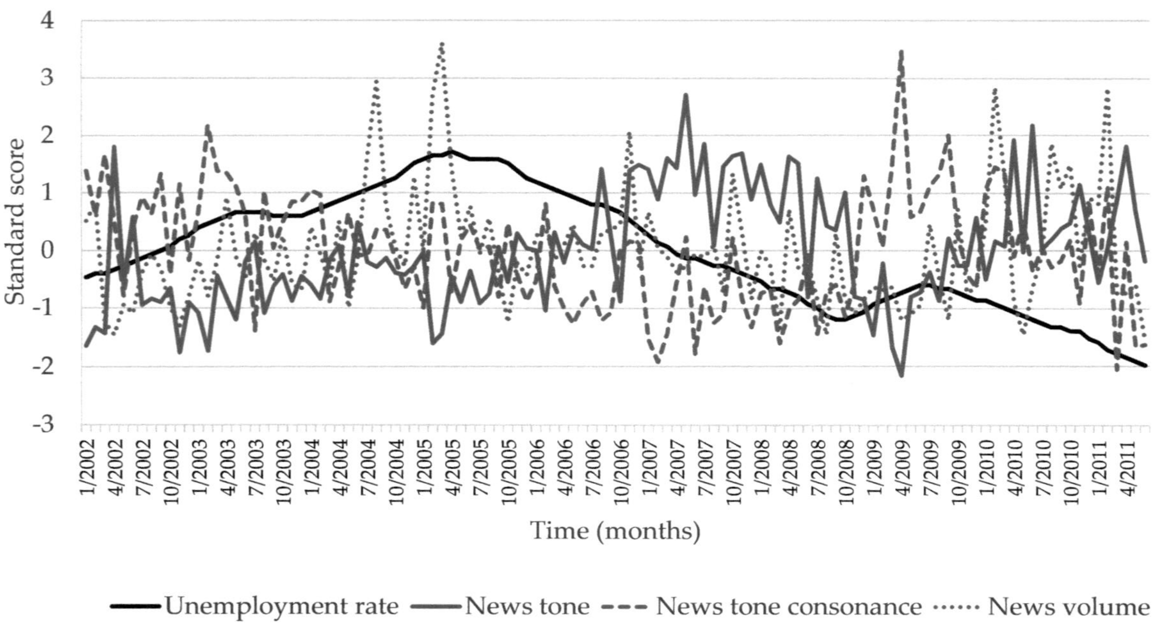

Figure 8: Unemployment rate and employment news

Notes. Observation period Jan 2002 – Jun 2011. All data are z-transformed. The recession periods comprise Q1 2003 to Q3 2004 and Q2 2008 to Q1 2009. News tone, consonance, and volume are monthly means and sums respectively of the total news on employment of four news outlets: *ARD Tagesschau, ZDF heute, RTL aktuell, BILD* (Lischka 2015, 382–85). The German unemployment rate is published by the German Federal Statistical Office and is adjusted for season. All data are z-transformed for combined display in one figure.

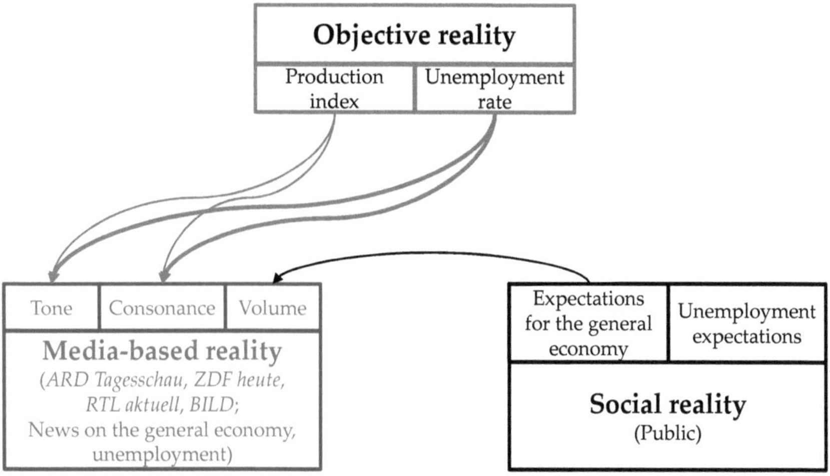

Figure 9: Main influences on media-based reality for news on the general economy and unemployment

Source: Compiled by the author based on results in Lischka (2015, 384, Table 1)

Note. Stronger influences are indicated with thicker arrows.

Results for news on the general economy partly confirm the doubt, expressed by the German journalists surveyed in the Worlds of Journalisms Study, that they had the ability to depict reality as it is (see Section 3.1). A reason that may explain a lack of a forecasting ability is that the general economic situation is more complex than one real-world economic indicator that was used for testing in the present study. News stories on a certain topic relate to more than one issue and do not always follow the aggregate real-world indicator. This becomes apparent in the stronger volatility of news tone and consonance in *Figures 7* and *8*. In addition, the topic of the general economy is less elusive than the topic of unemployment. To report on the general economy includes many further occasions and aspects that appear to be relevant for a journalist and therefore may be interpreted differently from what aggregate numbers would suggest—especially during the financial crisis period as suggested by Scheufele (2003) when news consonance on news on the general economy increases during the 2008/9 recession. Incoming economic news varies and requires specific selection and interpretation every day. Possibly, news relates to real-world economic events on a micro, meso, or macro level and therefore may deviate from the general, aggregate trend on a macro level. At the same time, these economic events "pay" into real-world economic indicators measured on a macro level—i.e., when a company gains strong returns or provides new jobs, these incidents may become part of the news. And they are also part of the production and unemployment numbers. This relationship may be closer for occasions to report on unemployment.

3.4 Interim summary and conclusions

Tracing the relation between objective and media economic reality as illustrated in *Figure 1* (path A), the following conclusion can be drawn from the review of this study's results against the theoretical background and previous research.

A. Economic news is unsurprisingly not a copy of the real-world *aggregate* economy yet is in alignment with it. Economic news presents a more diverse and therefore volatile picture of the economy than aggregate economic indicators suggest. As a matter of course, news on a particular economic topic also refers to real-world events on a micro or meso level which may deviate from the major aggregate economic trend on a macro level. That is, journalists and editors select real-world events for news coverage based on news factors and ascribed values, i.e., characteristics that are *event-internal*, but not based on the fit with the general aggregate economic situation. Therefore, economic indicators cannot fully predict short-term developments of news volume, tone, and consonance.

   In addition, the selection processes are determined by the specific situation of each journalist within each media organization which change after an orientation phase caused by the start of the financial crisis. This supports Scheufele's (2003) assumption that a crucial event can change journalistic interpretation. Therefore, news outlets start to differ in their *levels* of economic news tone, consonance, and volume more strongly after the start of the financial crisis. Yet, the news tone, consonance and volume *trends* between news outlets are mostly similar.

4 Economic news and economic sentiment

This chapter reviews how economic news coverage influences economic expectations. It is dedicated to answering the second research question, *How strongly does economic news influence both public and expert economic sentiment?*, which is related to path B in *Figure 1*. The role of economic news in economic expectations is explained in more detail in Lischka (2015, 378–80) concerning the public and Lischka and Siegert (2013, 175–76) concerning economic experts. Theory and literature are briefly summarized and the results of these studies are evaluated in Sections 4.1 and 4.2. In Section 4.3, the impact of economic news on expectations of the public and economic experts is compared applying an additional VAR analysis.

4.1 The role of economic news in the economic sentiment of the public

An individual's opinion on a certain topic is a result of direct experiences, the experiences of reference groups, interpersonal communication, one's own as well as other people's opinions, and media consumption (see e.g., Ball-Rokeach and DeFleur 1976; Gerbner 1969; McCombs and Shaw 1972; Schenk 1997; Scherer 1990). Some authors argue that news is the *major* information source of the public for perceiving the overall economic situation (Blinder and Krueger 2004; Goidel et al. 2010; Quiring and Weber 2012). In contrast, Haller and Norpoth (1997, 573) describe the economy as a "doorstep issue" that is accessible through real-world experience. Direct experience such as an increased budget at work, unemployed family members or friends, the bustle in the shopping mall or the amount of construction work in a city characterize cues that can all be perceived by non-specialists as indicators of a good or bad economic situation (Lischka 2015). Moreover, the personal financial situation can be taken as a cue for national economic conditions (Haller and Norpoth 1997, 569).

For the German public, TV and daily newspapers are the most important sources for current affairs (Ecke 2011, 19). In general, the interest in economic information of the German population as well as the range of economic news outlets have increased since the 1990s (Quiring 2004). According to a survey based on a representative sample of the German population (n = 960) in 2010/11, about 42% (44%) of the respondents were very strongly and strongly (moderately) interested in economic, finance, and business topics (Mast 2012, 132). Broadcast and print news followed by conversations with family, friends and colleagues were most often used information sources for economic issues (Mast 2012, 134). Online news sources were used occasionally on a weekly basis only. When asking respondents for naming their most often used news outlets used for economic information, *ARD Tagesschau* is named as number two and *BILD* as number ten of most often used news outlets (Mast 2012, 138).

As early as the mid-twentieth century, Katona (1975; 1957) emphasized the information-distributing effects of the media on economic attitudes. That economic news affects what and how individuals think about the economy has often been empirically proved. Media are not only an important source of economic knowledge for individuals, but they influence economic attitudes as well—as communication and economics research has shown (e.g., Bachl May 21-25, 2009; Blood and Phillips 1995; Brettschneider 2003; Doms and Morin 2004; Dräger 2011; Easaw and Ghoshray 2010; Goidel and Langley 1995; Goidel et al. 2010; Hagen 2005; Hester and Gibson 2003; Ju 2008; Lamla and Lein 2008; Soroka 2006; Tims, Fan, and Freeman 1989). Some studies find very small or smaller agenda-setting effects compared to effects of real-world cues (Behr and Iyengar 1985; Erbring, Goldenberg, and Miller 1980; Goidel et al. 2010; Haller and Norpoth 1997; Shehata and Strömbäck 2013; Wu et al. 2002). Also most recently, Kleinnijenhuis, Schultz, and Oegema (2015) show based on VAR model estimations that real-world stock market indicators (DOW, FTSE, DAX) were stronger predictors of consumer sentiment than increasing frame complexity of economic news during the financial crisis.

In general, the intensity of agenda-setting effects depends on communicator, message, recipient, and environmental or situational variables. Differences in news effects are due to the overall economic situation, tone or negativity, salience or obtrusiveness of the issue, the level of trust accorded to the news outlet (see discussion in Lischka 2015; for an overview see Cialdini 2001; Johnson, Maio, and Smith-McLallen 2005), or the level of interest in the economy (van Dalen et al. 05.02.2015). Non-obtrusive, sociotropic issues, which are not related to personal experience (Demers et al. 1989; Mutz 1992; Zucker 1978), are found to have stronger agenda-setting or cultivating effects than obtrusive or egocentric issues (Hetsroni and Lowenstein 2012). This is in line with the obtrusive contingency hypothesis stating that when people have experience with an issue rather develop expectations based on their own experiences than use media coverage to develop expectations (Demers et al. 1989; Lee 2004; see Lischka 2015, 378–79 for further discussion). However, although individuals experience unemployment themselves or vicariously through family and friends, this obtrusive or egocentric issue may only be regarded as an important public issue if it appears in the news. According to Mutz (1994, 708), news coverage exposes recipients to similar experiences and "should reassure many people that their problems and concerns are shared by many others." Only then can the extent of a problem be recognized, and expectations for unemployment in a country be developed. As a result, "heavy unemployment coverage also increases the extent to which perceptions of national unemployment conditions are generalized from personal experience" (Mutz 1994, 689). Stronger news effects on sociotropic perceptions—i.e., unemployment or the economy as *societal* problem, compared with egocentric perceptions, i.e., unemployment or the economy as *personal* problem—was described by Mutz (1992) and has been since then confirmed (Hagen May 27, 2004). In this regard, also the results of Goidel et al. (2010) indicate that sociotropic expectations for the long-term national economic development are more strongly affected by economic news tone and volume than personal financial evaluations and expectations.

Lischka (2015) analyses dynamic effects of economic indicators, economic expectations of the public, and news on the general economy as well as unemployment in Germany between 2002 to 2011. The observation period takes periods of economic expansion as well as recession into account as for example suggested by Blood and Phillips (1995). Effects are separately estimated for recession and non-recession times.

Results in Lischka (2015) reveal news effects on public expectations towards the general economy as well as towards unemployment as national, i.e., sociotropic, problems. However, public economic expectations are more strongly influenced by *real-world economic indicators* than by news coverage. That is, indicators of the objective reality better forecast the social reality than the media-based reality. This result is in line with previous research revealing that a change in public economic expectations "is in fact a function of individuals' reactions to the economy itself, rather than the effect of media coverage" (Soroka 2006, 380). Also Kleinnijenhuis, Schultz, and Oegema (2015) show that consumer confidence can better be forecast by real-world stock market indices than by frame complexity and news tone of economic news coverage. This also relates to Zerback, Koch, and Kramer's (2015) study revealing that explicit cues have greater effects than implicit cues on the public opinion. For unemployment, Soroka (2006) as well as Shehata and Strömbäck (2013) find *no* agenda-setting effects for the perceived importance of unemployment as a sociotropic "important political issue today," whereas the real-world unemployment rate has a forecasting ability. A stronger autoregression in the unemployment opinion, i.e., a stronger dependency on its own past, may prevent a news effect (Soroka 2006). Shehata and Strömbäck (2013) suppose that chronic accessibility due to continuously high news salience prevents a news effect. Tan and Weaver (2013) similarly state that agenda-setting effects are harder to produce for habituated issues due to increased information inertia or resistance to change attitudes as suggested by Saltiel and Woelfel (1975). The public expectations for the general economy and for unemployment used in Lischka (2015) reveal a mediocre autoregressive relation with its own past that is significant on the 10% level. Thus, the level of autoregression of the public opinion may be an indicator for habituation, which explains the absence of agenda-setting effects. The better forecasting ability of real-world indicators than news also indicates the importance of direct experience with the economy as well as interpersonal communication. In this regard, Kalogeropoulos et al. (2015) show that less interpersonal communication and fewer personal experiences with economic issues (e.g., job loss, cut of private expenses) are related to higher news effects on economic knowledge.

News tone on the general economy has some forecasting ability for public expectations, both for the general economy and for unemployment expectations, during the 2008/9 *recession,* which is in line with previous findings (Hester and Gibson 2003; Wu et al. 2002). The news tone effect on public expectations for the general economy increases with higher news volume. This relates to results by Golan and Wanta (2001) who show that news volume is a stronger predictor of public opinion than news tone. Surprisingly, higher news consonance does not lead to stronger news tone effects on the public, although it is found to be is necessary for collective media effects (see B in Chapter 2). But the results suggest a negative tendency in public expectations for the general economy, i.e., lower news consonance leads to stronger news tone effects (Lischka 2015, 386–87, Table 2). The lack of an indirect influence may be due to the high volatility of news consonance over time. Also, news volume and therefore news salience may be a clearer signal to the public, which may stimulate follow-up communication. On the other hand, lower news consonance may also increase the need for follow-up conversations that result in stronger alignment between the average news tone and public expectations during the 2008/9 recession. During non-recession times, the production index tends to forecast public expectations for the general economy. During non-recession times and the weaker 2003/4 recession, both economic indicators can forecast unemployment expectations.

Figure 10 summarizes the main influences on public expectations found in the analyses in Lischka (2015, 386–87, Table 2).

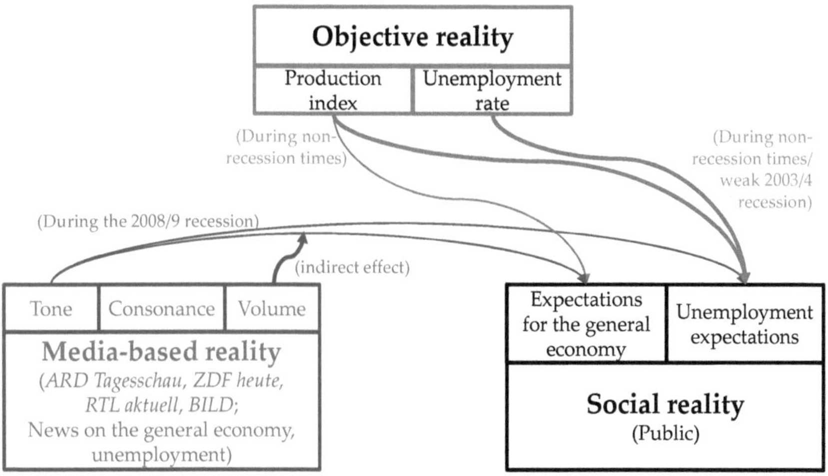

Figure 10: Main influences on public expectations for the general economy and unemployment

Source: Compiled by the author based on results in Lischka (2015, 386-387, Table 2)

Note. Stronger influences are indicated with thicker arrows.

To sum up, the second-level agenda-setting effect of news tone is moderated by an increased need for orientation (Matthes 2008) and news dependency (Ball-Rokeach and DeFleur 1976) as well as higher news salience during the recession. Hence, second-level agenda-setting effects depend on news quality *and* quantity. In addition, the public draws conclusions from the news on the general economy for both the general economy and unemployment expectations. This heuristic is in line with the economic cycle between the general state of the economy and the employment situation: employment numbers are a lagging indicator of the economy, i.e., result from changes in the general economy (Kater 2008). Thus, to describe agenda setting on a given topic, the inclusion of news that may not appear to be directly related to the given topic is required.

4.2 The role of economic news in the economic sentiment of economic experts

In this study, the agenda-setting effects discussed above are found for the public's economic expectations. When it comes to economic experts, agenda-setting effects may decline with decreasing media dependency, as discussed in Lischka and Siegert (2013, 175). This section examines the influence of news on experts' economic expectations based on the results of Lischka and Siegert (2013) and reflecting on third-person effects.

Economic experts depend less than does the public on news concerning the general state of the economy due to their professional experience with the economy as argued for example by Hagen (2005). One can assume that they are highly involved with economic aspects such as the development of the economy, corporate investments, and private consumption. According to a survey of German corporate decision makers (Mast 2012, 134), they use conversations with their personal environment more often as source for economic information than the public. However, corporate decision makers also use general- and special-interest news outlets more often than the public to inform themselves about economic issues (Mast 2012). Both, personal interactions and news consumption may cause agenda-setting effects (see discussion in Section 2.1, B). Furthermore, Nelissen, Konig, and Renckstorf (2008) show that news consumption corresponds with people's occupational position. People holding an executive role in a company pay more attention to news in order to understand current public affairs. Nelissen, Konig, and Renckstorf (2008) explain the greater news exposure of executives with a greater interest in politics and increased need for social networking. In addition, Mast (2012, 132) reveals a great interest of decision makers in economic topics. Almost 90% of surveyed corporate decision makers are very strongly and strongly interested in economic, finance, and business topics.

Experts may assume that consumers' and entrepreneurs' economic sentiment and behavior are affected by news. According to Kepplinger's (2007) model of reciprocal effects, news reports serve as cues for decision makers to assume media effects on the public and estimate public opinion. To estimate public opinion, results from opinion polls, media reports, expert analysis, and own impressions can be used (Kepplinger 2007, 12). To assess economic decision making in the total population, economic experts may use general news to get an idea about public opinion. To assess future private consumption, general news may be a good source for understanding or coming to conclusions on consumer sentiment (see discussion in Lischka and Siegert 2013, 176). Experts might expect that news affects or reflects the public opinion according to the effect of presumed influence (Gunther and Storey 2003). An assumed news effect on other people increases with social distance "as the 'others' become more socially remote from the perceiver" (Tewksbury 2002, 247)—which may apply to the experts' perception of the general public.

Hence, for the audience group consisting of economic experts, the media dependency model (Ball-Rokeach and DeFleur 1976) in combination with the effect of presumed influence (Gunther and Storey 2003) as a third-person effect (Davison 1983) can explain news effects on experts. The theory of the effect of presumed influence proposes that people presume that others will act based on the perceived influence of the media. The media dependency approach suggests that news effects are more likely to occur when no direct experiences can be accessed. Third-person effects are found to be stronger with large, socially distant groups (Davison 1983; Perloff 1993; Tewksbury 2002). Experts may be more able to assess entrepreneurial behavior than consumer behavior as the latter comprises a large, socially distant group.

Lischka and Siegert (2013) estimated the influence of public-service economic news on experts' economic sentiment of the ifo World Economic Survey. The surveyed experts are professionals of multinational companies or researchers in economic institutes, i.e., "economists in managerial or research functions" (ifo 2014b). A notably difference between professionals and researchers is that professionals have more direct access to the situation in their company and within their sector, which may bias their overall expectations of the general economic development, and of consumer or investment behavior on country level. In addition, expectations of professionals within business-to-business sectors as opposed to business-to-consumer sectors may systematically vary as well. Eventually, professionals of companies operating on the durables versus consumer goods markets may arrive at different expectations. In addition, previous research revealed divergent estimates of economic parameters in a survey of academic economists, which correlated with economists' individual values (Fuchs, Krueger, and Poterba 1998). In a survey of members of the academic American Economic Association, Fuller and Geide-Stevenson (2003) find that a high consensus among scholars on economic propositions is concentrated in the area of international economics, whereas there is substantial to no consensus on macro- and microeconomic topics. For example, no consensus existed for the proposition stating that there are short- but no long-term effects of changes in aggregate demand on GDP. These studies suggest a separation of managerial and academic economists and even further subclassifications. Unfortunately, neither a breakdown of surveyed experts by organizational characteristics nor including the degree of consensus was possible for the present estimations.

Results of Lischka and Siegert (2013) reveal that the German experts' assessment of *present and future* private consumption expenditures relies on news tone of the past quarter of two Public-service evening TV news shows from Q3 2007 onward.[24] Before Q3 2007, news tone Granger causes the evaluation of the *present* state of the economy with lower forecasting ability and the *present* state of private consumption with higher forecasting ability, with a delay of one quarter. Because the real-world state of the economy also depends on the development of real-world private consumption whose evaluation in turn depends on news tone for the

24 The study estimates the effect of Swiss and German public-service news tone and volume on Swiss and German economic experts surveyed by the Ifo World Economic Survey. These are experts in economic institutions, universities, central banks, and multinational companies in each surveyed country (ifo 2014a). No effects are found for Swiss news on Swiss experts, which may be due to differences in German and Swiss economic news volume, tone, and topics.

experts, news tone also tends to Granger cause the evaluation of the general state of the economy. In contrast, the evaluation of present and future corporate investments is not in a Granger-causal relationship with news before Q3 2007. Only from Q3 2007 onward does the *ZDF heute* news tone tend to Granger cause the assessment of present investments. For these aspects of the economy, experts rely more on their own experiences than on news. The main results for experts' evaluations and expectations for corporate investments and private consumption expenditures are illustrated in *Figure 11*.

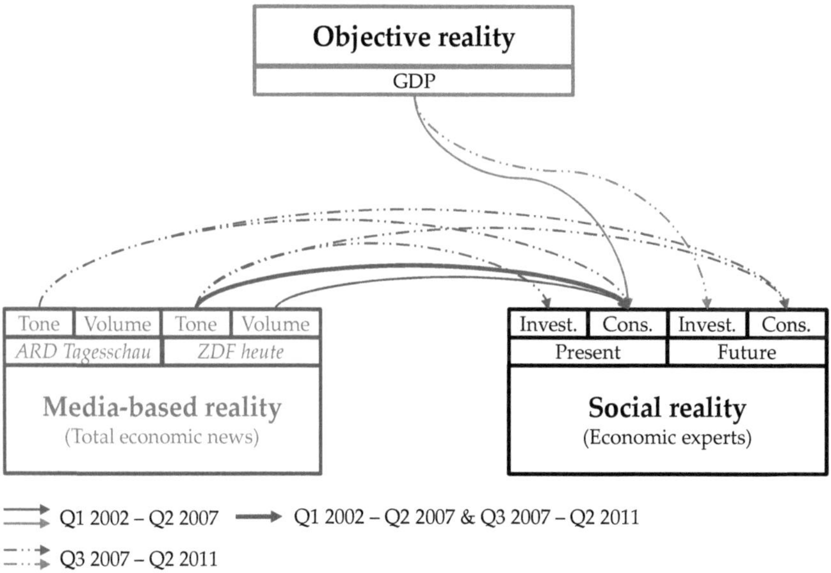

Figure 11: Main influences on experts' assessment of investments and consumption

Source: Compiled by the author based on results in Lischka and Siegert (2013, 180, Tabelle 2).

To conclude, the experts' dependency on news is higher in times of economic instability and when the news concerns the hard-to-predict behavior of the general public. Hence, results of Lischka and Siegert (2013) can be explained with the concepts of the third-person effect and media dependency.

Taking potential differences in expectation formation of professionals of various sectors into account, greater third-person effects can be expected for professionals in business-to-consumer than business-to-business sectors. For example, a survey of decision makers of major companies in Germany by Kepplinger (2010) shows a stronger effect of assumed media reactions on decisions made in companies in the business-to-consumer than business-to-business sectors. That is, major companies in consumer industries expect that media reports about their imminent decisions and take these potential reports into account. Thus, economic news may also play a greater role for end customer-related decisions in business-to-consumer than in business-to-business sectors. Section 5.2 takes industry differences into account when analyzing news effects on advertising expenditures.

4.3 Comparison of economic news effects on the public and economic experts

When comparing public and expert beliefs and views of the economy, Blendon et al. (1997) demonstrate that the public perceives the economy as performing less well and is more pessimistic about the future development than economists and attributes it to different reasons than economists do. For example, the public agrees to reasons such as, "the top executives are paid too much", "the federal deficit is too big", and "too many people are on welfare" (Blendon et al. 1997, 113–14). The authors explain the discrepancy with personal experiences of individuals that do not mirror official data, such as the buying activity people see in stores, a mistrust in official data, a negative tendency in news reports, and a lack of economic knowledge of the public. Blendon et al. (1997, 116) also ascribe a bias of the more privileged position of economists to their more optimistic economic expectations. This explanation as well as the previously mentioned result that economists' values correlate with policy positions (Fuchs, Krueger, and Poterba 1998) suggest a subjective evaluation of the economy also by experts.

When one compares the second-level agenda-setting effects of the news on the general public (Lischka 2015) with their effects on economic experts (Lischka and Siegert 2013), surprisingly, news effects appear to be stronger with economic experts than with the general public as explained variance (adjusted R^2) suggests. Whereas news tone can account for the variance of experts' evaluation of future private consumption, explaining up to 70% of that variance after 2007 (Lischka and Siegert 2013, 180, Tabelle 2), not more than 30% of variance is explained in the models treating public expectations (Lischka 2015, 386-387, Table 2). First, different observation periods may have caused the differences in results. Second, economic news on the general economy and on unemployment were estimated separately over the four major news outlets in Lischka (2015) whereas Lischka and Siegert (2013) took account of the entirety of economic news in two public-service news outlets. The following analysis will adjust these differences. A third technical explanation for this difference may be the data frequency. Agenda-setting effects on the general public were estimated using a data frequency of one month, and for experts using a quarterly frequency. A greater aggregation of data can cause greater effect sizes (Maurer 2004 on media effects; Lischka and Seufert 2015, 529–31 on the advertising sales relation). However, in order to not ignore agenda-setting effects occurring within one month and to show a more accurate picture, the data frequency will not be aggregated to quarters.

Hence, for a direct comparison, the VAR models used in Lischka (2015) are adapted to the VAR models used in Lischka and Siegert (2013, 179) in terms of scope (total economic news volume (*NV*) and tone (*NT*) of the two German public-service news outlets separately, omitting news consonance). The VAR models[25] for the public and experts' evaluations and expectations (*E*) including GDP (*GDP*) can be written as follows.

(2a) $\Delta E_t = \alpha_1 + \beta_1 \Delta E_{t-1} + \lambda_1 \Delta NT_{t-1} + \varsigma_1 \Delta NV_{t-2} + \gamma_1 \Delta GDP_{t-1} + \varepsilon_{1t}$

with α being the constant, β, λ, ς, γ being the coefficients and ε_t being the residuals. The resulting explained variance of *E* (adjusted R^2) of (2a) is compared with the explained variance of the following VAR model (3a) that omits news tone and volume.

(3a) $\Delta E_t = \alpha_1 + \beta_1 \Delta E_{t-1} + \gamma_1 \Delta GDP_{t-1} + \varepsilon_{1t}$

The questions of the experts' and public's estimation of the future development of the general economy are quite similar and can be compared. Additionally, the public's judgment on the general economy during the last 12 months and the experts' evaluation of the present state of the economy are used to compare news effects on retrospective and present evaluations versus expectations. The evaluation and expectation questions for

25 Since only to explain evaluations and expectations (*E*) is of interest, the remaining equations of the VAR model are omitted.

the general public were, respectively: "How do you think the general economic situation in the country has changed over the past 12 months?" and "How do you expect the general economic situation in this country to develop over the next 12 months?" (European Commission 2014, 47; Lischka 2015, 386). The evaluation and expectation questions for experts were, respectively: [Give us your opinion on] "this country's general situation regarding overall economy, present judgment" and [Tell us what you expect] "from now on: expected situation by the end of the next 6 months" (Lischka and Siegert 2013, 182, Appendix 1). Besides the time horizon in the question, the data collection methods differ for the two surveys: face-to-face interviews for the public, paper and pencil questionnaires for the experts; and the survey frequencies as well: monthly and quarterly respectively.

The data in monthly frequency used in the VAR model for the public are converted to standard deviations and displayed, combined, in *Figure 12*. The standard deviations in the public evaluations and expectations develop similarly and in line with the real production index until they reach a peak in the middle of 2007. From the middle of 2007 onward, public expectations are more pessimistic than evaluations or the production index until mid-2009, when expectations are slightly more positive than evaluations. Standard deviations in news tone of the *ARD Tagesschau* and *ZDF heute* are comparably volatile but develop in line with public evaluations except for 2011. News volume shows a strong increase—up to four standard deviations—when the production index starts to decline from the end of 2008 until the end of 2010, after which the production index once again reveals positive standard deviations.

The data in quarterly frequency used in the VAR model for the experts are converted to standard deviations and displayed in *Figure 13*. The expert evaluations develop similarly to the news tone of both outlets except for 2011. Therefore, expert and public evaluations seem to be similar. But the expert expectations become negative in 2006 what is one year earlier than the expectations of the general public. While the GDP develops positively until 2008, experts have started expecting a negative development two years in advance. This sentiment is not in line with any other data series in *Figure 13*. Instead, the expert expectations for the general economy develop in an anti-cyclical manner compared with their evaluations and the GDP.

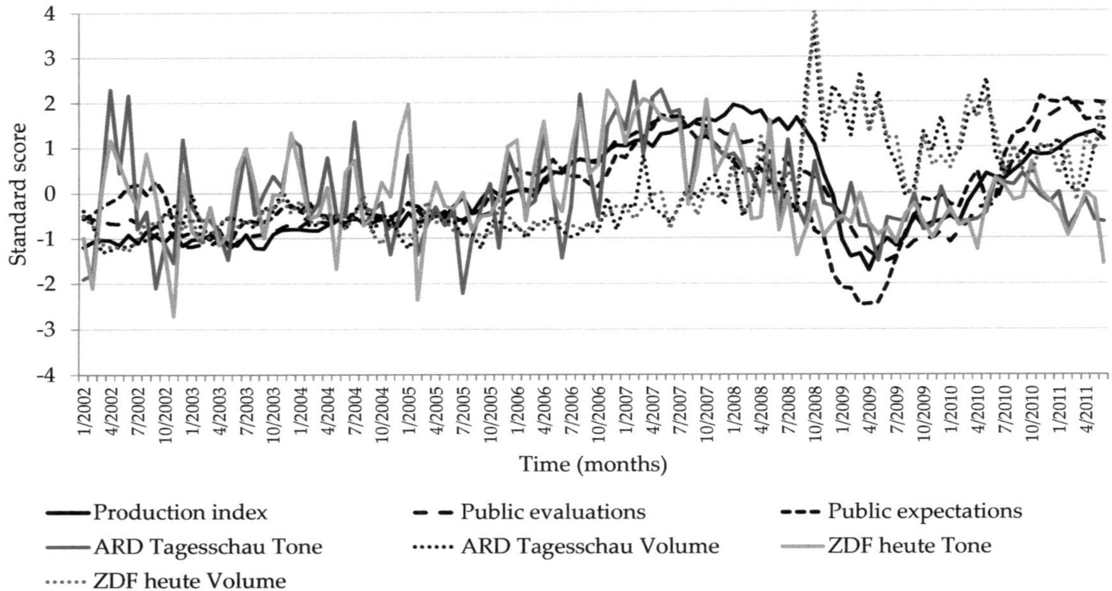

Figure 12: The production index, public sentiment and public-service economic news

Notes. Observation period Jan 2002–Jun 2011. All data are z-transformed. The break date is Jan 2007. Public evaluations: "How do you think the general economic situation in the country has changed over the past 12 months?" Public expectations: "How do you expect the general economic situation in this country to develop over the next 12 months?" (European Commission and Directorate-General for Economic and Financial Affairs 2007, p. 47; Lischka in review, p. 13). News tone and volume are monthly means and sums respectively of the *total* economic news per outlet. The production index is published by the German Federal Statistical Office and is adjusted for working day and season. All data are z-transformed for combined display in one figure.

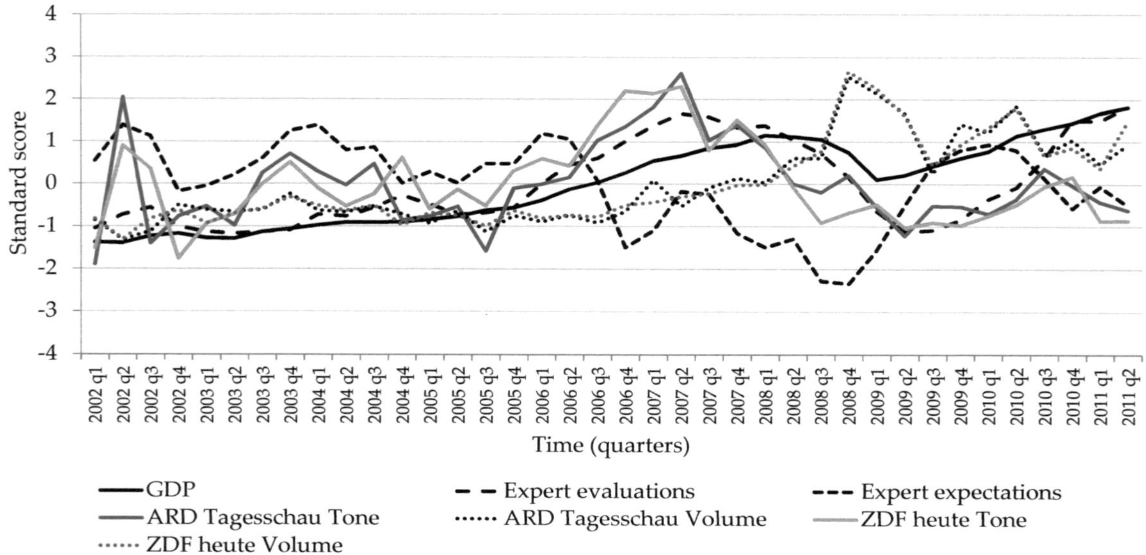

Figure 13: The GDP, expert sentiment and public-service economic news

Notes. Observation period Q1 2002 – Q2 2011. All data are z-transformed. The break date is Q1 2007. Expert evaluation and expectation, respectively: "This country's general situation regarding overall economy present judgment" and "from now on: expected situation by the end of the next 6 months" (Lischka and Siegert 2013, 182, Appendix 1). News tone and volume are quarterly means and sums respectively of the *total* economic news per outlet. The German GDP is published by Eurostat and is adjusted for working day and season.

VAR results as displayed in Table 2 reveal that the public's expectations for and evaluations of the general economy are influenced by economic news. Before 2007, public *evaluations* can be better forecast from *ZDF heute* news tone than public expectations. From 2007 onward, the public *expectations* tend to rely more strongly on *ZDF heute* news than public evaluations. Up to four lags (four months) of *ZDF heute* tone and volume affect public expectations. However, *ZDF heute* news tone Granger causes evaluations and expectations only by trend from 2007 onward but significantly before 2007. In addition, from 2007 onward, *ARD Tagesschau* news of the previous month and the development of the production index three months ago influences public evaluations and expectations. This indicates an increased awareness toward real-world economic indicators and a slighter but longer lasting awareness toward public-service news in the times of the financial crisis. Hence, the public absorbs economic information from various sources during the times of the financial crisis in order to understand the current state of the economy and to develop economic expectations.

In contrast, economic experts predominantly rely on news only for their evaluation of the *present* economic situation. The news tone of *ZDF heute* Granger causes the experts' evaluation of the *present* state of the economy, which also tends to be stronger from 2007 onward. Comparing economic expectations of the public versus those of economic experts, the latter are hardly influenced by economic news. An increase in economic news volume in the *ARD Tagesschau* has some forecasting ability at a 10% significance level for an increase in optimistic expectations of the experts before 2007. News tone does not Granger cause expert expectations, whereas news tone of *ZDF heute* Granger causes public expectations for both observation periods.[26] During economically insecure times, from 2007 onward, expert expectations do not rely on news but public ones do. For economic experts, the GDP development has a forecasting ability for economic evaluations and expectations from 2007 onward, which is similar to the public. In the times of the financial crisis, economic experts raised their awareness toward real-world economic indicators.

26 Limited direct comparability due to monthly versus quarterly data frequency. However, when estimating this relationship on a quarterly frequency for the public, the impact of *ZDF heute* news tone on public expectations from 2007 onward lasting four months should become evident.

Table 2: Influence of public-service economic news on public and expert sentiment for the general economy

Dependent variable	Public: Evaluations (*E*) (last 12 months)	Public: Expectations (*E*) (next 12 months)	Economic experts[1]: Evaluations (*E*) (present)	Economic experts[1]: Expectations (*E*) (next 6 months)
	Jan 2002 – Jun 2007		Q1 2002 – Q2 2007	
ARD Tagesschau				
Granger causality (*F*)				
$NT \rightarrow E$	n.s.	n.s.	8.06*	n.s.
$NV \rightarrow E$	n.s.	n.s.	n.s.	3.62°
adjusted R^2	-0.01	-0.06	0.40	0.10
Share of adj. R^2 *NT* and *NV*	-0.05	-0.04	0.29	0.14
Influence factors	n.s.	n.s.	$NT_{t-1}+^{*}$	$NV_{t-1}+^{\circ}$
ZDF heute				
Granger causality (*F*)				
$NT \rightarrow E$	4.20*	2.81*	3.37°	n.s.
$NV \rightarrow E$	n.s.	n.s.	n.s.	n.s.
adjusted R^2	0.19	0.09	0.19	0.32
Share of adj. R^2 *NT* and *NV*	0.15	0.10	0.08	-0.08
Influence factors	$NT_{t-1}+^{**}$, $_{t-2}+^{*}$	$NT_{t-1}+^{**}$, $NV_{t-1}+^{\circ}$	$NT_{t-1}+^{\circ}$	n.s.
	Jul 2007 – Jun 2011		Q3 2007 – Q2 2011	
ARD Tagesschau				
Granger causality (*F*)				
$NT \rightarrow E$	n.s.	n.s.	n.s.	n.s.
$NV \rightarrow E$	2.40°	n.s.	n.s.	n.s.
adjusted R^2	0.55	0.31	0.52	0.22
Share of adj. R^2 *NT* and *NV*	0.11	0.17	0.01	-0.08
Influence factors	$NV_{t-1}-^{*}$, $Prod_{t-3}+^{*}$	$NT_{t-1}+^{*}$, $Prod_{t-3}+^{\circ}$	n.s.	$GDP_{t-1}-^{\circ}$
ZDF heute				
Granger causality (*F*)				
$NT \rightarrow E$	2.26°	2.55°	3.55°	n.s.
$NV \rightarrow E$	n.s.	n.s.	4.84°	n.s.
adjusted R^2	0.57	0.56	0.67	0.31
Share of adj. R^2 *NT* and *NV*	0.13	0.22	0.16	0.00
Influence factors	$NT_{t-1}+^{**}$, $_{t-4}-^{\circ}$, $Prod_{t-3}+^{*}$	$NT_{t-1}+^{**}$, $_{t-2}+^{\circ}$, $_{t-3}+^{\circ}$, $_{t-4}+^{\circ}$, $NV_{t-1}-^{\circ}$, $_{t-2}-^{*}$, $_{t-3}-^{*}$, $Prod_{t-3}+^{*}$	$NT_{t-1}+^{\circ}$, $NV_{t-1}-^{*}$, $GDP_{t-1}+^{*}$	$GDP_{t-1}-^{\circ}$

(Continues on the next page)

Table 2, continued

Notes. For Granger causality, the null hypotheses that the coefficients on all the lags of an endogenous variable are jointly zero is tested. Line "influence factors" contains the lags and signs of significant VAR coefficients. Data frequency public: monthly, experts: quarterly, i.e., *t*-1 is equivalent to one month/one quarter for public/expert columns, respectively.

1 As published in Lischka and Siegert (2013, Tabelle 2, column 4). The VAR models are controlled by the production index (Prod, monthly measurement of the GDP, public) or the GDP (experts); n.s.: not significant, °: significant on 10% level, *: significant on 5% level, **: significant on 1% level.

News tone (*NT*) and volume (*NV*) are monthly/quarterly means and sums respectively of the *total* economic news per outlet. Public evaluations: "How do you think the general economic situation in the country has changed over the past 12 months?," public expectations: "How do you expect the general economic situation in this country to develop over the next 12 months?" (European Commission and Directorate-General for Economic and Financial Affairs 2007, p. 47; Lischka in review, p. 13). Expert evaluation and expectation respectively: "This country's general situation regarding overall economy present judgment" and "from now on: expected situation by the end of the next 6 months" (Lischka and Siegert 2013, 182, Appendix 1).

Hence, news stimuli may be used for updating specific economic sentiments by both groups as media dependency varies across the two groups and over time. Whereas the public depends more strongly on economic news for understanding the future, especially in insecure times, experts are not guided by general economic news to develop their economic expectations.

4.4 Interim summary and conclusions

Tracing the relation between the media-generated and social economic realities as illustrated in *Figure 1* (path B), the following interim conclusion can be drawn from the discussion of these study's results against the theoretical background and previous research.

B. Both the public and economic experts are more likely to use information gathered from their daily lives to develop economic sentiment on sociotropic economic issues than information gathered from the general news. This result is in line with Haller and Norpoth (1997, 573) calling the economy a "doorstep issue," which is accessible through real-world cues. The level of autoregression of the public opinion for an economic issue may be an indicator for the habituation of an issue or *information inertia*, which can explain the absence of agenda-setting effects. Yet economic news coverage has some effects on collective economic sentiment. These effects are stronger in economically *insecure* times. The overall economic situation is an important condition for news effects as media dependency varies with it. Therefore, the news indicates whether an economic situation should be perceived as a social *problem* as suggested by Mutz (1992) and discussed by Katona (1968).

While the ability of news to forecast the public opinion can be considered a causal effect in line with the theory of the persuasive press inference (Gunther 1998), the ability of news tone to forecast the expert opinion is based on the influence of presumed influence (Gunther and Storey 2003). While the public may take economic news as a depiction of the real world, especially in uncertain economic times, economic experts consider public opinion *and* behavior as influenced by economic news as economic news tone can forecast the expert expectations for private consumption. Therefore, results suggest that economic experts expect that the public will behave according to implicit cues in economic news.

5 Economic news, economic sentiment and economic behavior

This chapter answers the third research question, *Does economic news influence private and corporate economic behavior?*, and relates to path C in *Figure 1*. Section 5.1 focuses on public economic behavior using the example of purchase intention. Section 5.2 addresses corporate economic behavior using the example of advertising expenditures.

5.1 Private economic behavior: Purchase intention

This part revises the literature on the relation between public economic sentiment and consumption behavior in Section 5.1.1 and extends the discussion including the role of economic news for behavior in Section 5.1.2. An additional empirical analysis on the temporal relationship between purchase intention, economic expectations and economic news is presented in Sections 5.1.3 and 5.1.4.

5.1.1 The influence of public economic sentiment on private economic behavior

Katona can be considered a pioneer introducing the human factor to economics by emphasizing the ability of economic attitudes to predict economic behavior. In Katona's view, consumer sentiment cannot be explained only by real-world economic and financial variables—because "[n]ot every income increase brings forth a feeling of satisfaction or of advance in financial well-being" (Katona 1957, 121)—but is a complex result, an "intermediary variable between the numerous pieces of information consumers digest, the stimuli, and the expenditure decision" (Vuchelen 2004, 495). The purchase of goods is affected by (1) experiences and expectations for people's own financial situation, (2) direct and indirect experiences for the general economic outlook, and (3) people's ability to buy (e.g., changes in income, liquid assets, debts, access to credits, possessions) (Katona 1957, 124; 1974, 22). Hence, consumer sentiment contains information beyond real-world economic indicators. In addition, news may affect intangible psychological factors such as optimism, pessimism, or uncertainty that are part of the willingness to spend (Katona 1975). This idea to describe behavioral intentions is in line with communication scholars reasoning that public opinion is a result of direct and indirect experiences, one's own opinion, and media consumption (see e.g., Ball-Rokeach and DeFleur 1976; Gerbner 1969; McCombs and Shaw 1972; Schenk 1997; Scherer 1990).

Empirical testing has often proven the forecasting ability of consumer sentiment for aggregate consumption (see overview in Eppright, Arguea, and Huth 1998; Vuchelen 2004). Chua and Tsiaplias (2009) show that consumer sentiment data provide information not available through historical consumption. However, the forecasting ability of consumer sentiment often declines but remains statistically significant when controlling with macroeconomic data (Carroll, Fuhrer, and Wilcox 1994; Fuhrer 1993; Ludvigson 2004; Mishkin 1978) or leading economic indicators such as interest rates (Ivanova and Lahiri 2001). Consumer sentiment is found to be cointegrated with real consumption and Granger cause consumption with a time lag of four to five months (Gelper, Lemmens, and Croux 2007) or up to three quarters (Praet and Vuchelen 1984). Especially in times of higher uncertainty and stronger volatility in consumer sentiment, the consumer sentiment forecasting ability is strong (Desroches and Gosselin 2004; Ivanova and Lahiri 2001). Based on the consumer survey of the European Commission, Praet and Vuchelen (1984) certify changes in the German consumer sentiment an explained variance of about 75% for changes in real consumption. Cotsomitis and Kwan (2006) assess that economic expectations have forecasting ability for German consumption whereas the total Consumer Confidence Index of the European Commission does not. Beyond that, forecasting ability varies strongly among European countries.

The forecasting ability of consumer sentiment components varies across goods (Ludvigson 2004; Wilcox 2007). According to Katona (1957), the purchase of durable goods is more closely related to the evaluation of people's current and prospective financial situation than to income increases. In empirical studies, consumption of goods is often classified into services, non-durable, and durable goods according to the Fair (2004) Macroeconometric model of the US economy. Many studies confirm the ability of consumer sentiment to forecast the consumption of durable goods or, more specifically, of cars, trucks and motorbikes (Adrangi and Macri 2011; Easaw, Garratt, and Heravi 2005; Easaw and Heravi 2004; Ivanova and Lahiri 2001; Ludvigson 2004; Mishkin 1978). However, conflicting results are found as well. For goods excluding automotive and services, the University of Michigan's Index of Consumer Sentiment (ICS)[27] improves forecasting of consumption (Carroll, Fuhrer, and Wilcox 1994). The ICS has more predictive power for the consumption of services than for that of durables or non-durables (Gelper, Lemmens, and Croux 2007). In addition, ICS component questions are found to forecast durables, non-durable, and service consumption whereas the overall ICS index is found to forecast only non-durable consumption (Wilcox 2007).

Using a consumer confidence index or its individual components leads to differences in results. According to Wilcox (2007), the best forecasting ability is offered by the evaluation of family finances and buying conditions (good or bad time to buy major household items) for consumption as opposed to the evaluation of the economic conditions and a sentiment index. The financial situation turned out to improve forecasting of the consumption of non-durable and economic expectations the automobile consumption (Wilcox 2007). In a four-quarter-ahead model, ICS and all components can forecast consumption of durables and automobiles. The evaluation of the right time to purchase, the personal financial situation expectations and national economic expectations have the greatest

27 The ICS includes questions that are very similar to the Consumer Survey of the European Commission (2014). The components of ICS as reported in Starr (2012, 1110) are as follows. Q1: "We are interested in how people are getting along financially these days. Would you say that you (and your family living there) are better off or worse off financially than you were a year ago?" Q2: "Now looking ahead—do you think that a year from now you (and your family living there) will be better off financially, or worse off, or just about the same as now?" Q3: "Now turning to business conditions in the country as a whole—do you think that during the next 12 months we will have good times financially, or bad times, or what?" Q4: "Looking ahead, which would you say is more likely—that in the country as a whole we will have continuous good times during the next 5 years or so, or that we will have periods of widespread unemployment or depression, or what?" Q5: "About the big things people buy for their homes—such as furniture, a refrigerator, stove, television, and things like that. Generally speaking, do you think now is a good or bad time for people to buy major household items?"

forecasting ability. Economic *expectations* prove to be more powerful consumer sentiment components than the evaluation of *current* economic conditions. Yet in a one-quarter-ahead model, private consumption of durables or automobiles cannot be forecast by ICS or any of its components (Wilcox 2007).

Although previous results vary according to observation periods, countries, indices, and estimated models, previous research shows that a breakdown of a consumer sentiment index into its components and a breakdown of aggregate consumption into goods can provide useful insights. In addition, consumption may be able to forecast purchase intention. After a purchase, the intention to purchase the same good declines. Hence, current possessions affect purchase intention (Katona 1957) and need to be checked when estimating the attitude-behavior relation.

This means that a close relationship between economic sentiment and the public's behavior can be assumed. Therefore, an additional analysis on the relation between economic news, economic expectations, and purchase intention is conducted in the following sections. Beforehand, the role of news on economic behavior is discussed with previous and own research.

5.1.2 The influence of economic news and public economic sentiment on private economic behavior

Grossarth-Maticek and Mayr (2008) find that the counts of the word "recession" in German newspapers have a forecasting ability for the German GDP. This is in line with the idea that belief shocks (Salyer and Sheffrin 1998) or agents' self-fulfilling expectations (Farmer 1999; Harrison and Weder 2006) move the economy. In this regard, false announcements of the macroeconomic development can have an effect on economic growth (Oh and Waldman 1990).

Many studies indicate that economic news directly and indirectly affect economic behavior. Uhl (2012) finds that TV news tone and consumer sentiment can forecast private consumption with TV news being the slightly stronger variable. A model containing TV news tone, personal income and savings was the best combination to forecast private consumption in the USA. Goidel et al. (2010) show that personal financial expectations, which are supposed to affect consumption, strongly correlate with economic indicators and also slightly with economic news tone and volume in national TV. In contrast, an early study of Adoni and Cohen (1978) shows almost no influence of news on behavior.

> Economic news had almost no influence on the respondents in terms of their purchasing and saving habits. (...) only 10 percent of the respondents claimed to be taking the recommendations transmitted via economic news seriously and purchasing less, controlling for changes in the respondents' real income. (Adoni and Cohen 1978, 66–67)

More recently, Starr (2012) estimates a structural VAR model (SVAR) allowing economic news to affect consumer sentiment and spending. Economic news was measured as the share of respondents of the University of Michigan's Survey of Consumers mentioning favorable news, minus the share mentioning unfavorable news. This approach to measuring *perceived* news coverage is unlike the studies previously mentioned in Chapter 3, which apply content analyses to economic news. Starr's (2012) results reveal that, first, perceived news tone explains short-term fluctuations at a six-to-twelve month horizon in the ICS when the news tone moves unexpectedly, relative to economic data. Second, consumer sentiment has a small positive effect on consumer spending, which is in accordance with the results presented in Section 5.1.1. Third, unexpected changes in perceived news tone change aggregate consumption modestly. Thus, only strong deviations in economic news can affect private economic behavior.

Lischka's (2015, 389, Table 3) results for German news outlets reveal that public expectations for the general economy forecast real-world economic developments, whereas news does not have an unconditional direct effect on the real-world economy. The conclusion is either that the public makes correct assumptions regarding economic development or that the public influences the economy via economic decision making (Lischka 2015). The latter would be the case if private consumption depended on public economic expectations. If public expectations for the general economy affect people's purchase behavior, which in turn forecasts an aggregate economic indicator, then the public expectations influence the economy via private economic decision making. The next section provides a corresponding analysis extending the model estimated in Lischka (2015).

5.1.3 Data and measurement

The monthly consumer survey of the European Commission asks respondents similar questions as in the ICS about the general purchase evaluation with the question, "In view of the general economic situation, do you think that now it is the right moment for people to make major purchases such as furniture, electrical/electronic devices, etc.?" (*RM*) and purchase intention, "Compared to the past 12 months, do you expect to spend more or less money on major purchases (furniture, electrical/electronic devices, etc.) over the next 12 months?" (*PI*), the household's financial situation, "How do you expect the financial position of your household to change over the next 12 months?" (*FS*), and price trend expectations, "By comparison with the past 12 months, how do you expect that consumer prices will develop in the next 12 months?" (*PT*) (European Commission 2014, 48). Whether *RM, PI, FS,* or *PT* are influenced by economic news (*NT, NC, NV*) and public economic expectations (*PE*), will be tested by including *RM, PI, FS,* and *PT* to the VAR model to explain economic indicators (*EI*) used in Lischka (2015). The extended VAR model[28] has the form

(4a) $\Delta PE_t = \alpha_1 + \beta_1 \Delta PE_{t-n} + \lambda_{12} \Delta EI_{t-n} + \lambda_{13} \Delta FS_{t-n} + \lambda_{14} \Delta PT_{t-n} + \lambda_{15} \Delta RM_{t-n} + \lambda_{16} \Delta PI_{t-n} + \lambda_{17} NT_{t-n} + \lambda_{18} NC_{t-n} + \lambda_{19} NV_{t-n} + \varepsilon_t$

(4b) $\Delta FS_t = \alpha_2 + \beta_2 \Delta FS_{t-n} + \lambda_{22} \Delta EI_{t-n} + \lambda_{23} \Delta PE_{t-n} + \lambda_{24} \Delta PT_{t-n} + \lambda_{25} \Delta RM_{t-n} + \lambda_{26} \Delta PI_{t-n} + \lambda_{27} NT_{t-n} + \lambda_{28} NC_{t-n} + \lambda_{29} NV_{t-n} + \varepsilon_t$

(4c) $\Delta PT_t = \alpha_3 + \beta_3 \Delta PT_{t-n} + \lambda_{32} \Delta EI_{t-n} + \lambda_{33} \Delta FS_{t-n} + \lambda_{34} \Delta PE_{t-n} + \lambda_{35} \Delta RM_{t-n} + \lambda_{36} \Delta PI_{t-n} + \lambda_{37} NT_{t-n} + \lambda_{38} NC_{t-n} + \lambda_{39} NV_{t-n} + \varepsilon_t$

(4d) $\Delta RM_t = \alpha_4 + \beta_4 \Delta RM_{t-n} + \lambda_{42} \Delta EI_{t-n} + \lambda_{43} \Delta FS_{t-n} + \lambda_{44} \Delta PE_{t-n} + \lambda_{45} \Delta PT_{t-n} + \lambda_{46} \Delta PI_{t-n} + \lambda_{47} NT_{t-n} + \lambda_{48} NC_{t-n} + \lambda_{49} NV_{t-n} + \varepsilon_t$

(4e) $\Delta PI_t = \alpha_5 + \beta_5 \Delta PI_{t-n} + \lambda_{52} \Delta EI_{t-n} + \lambda_{53} \Delta FS_{t-n} + \lambda_{54} \Delta PE_{t-n} + \lambda_{55} \Delta RM_{t-n} + \lambda_{56} \Delta PT_{t-n} + \lambda_{57} NT_{t-n} + \lambda_{58} NC_{t-n} + \lambda_{59} NV_{t-n} + \varepsilon_t$

(4f) $\Delta EI_t = \alpha_6 + \beta_6 \Delta EI_{t-n} + \lambda_{62} \Delta PE_{t-n} + \lambda_{63} \Delta FS_{t-n} + \lambda_{64} \Delta PT_{t-n} + \lambda_{65} \Delta RM_{t-n} + \lambda_{66} \Delta PI_{t-n} + \lambda_{67} NT_{t-n} + \lambda_{68} NC_{t-n} + \lambda_{69} NV_{t-n} + \varepsilon_t$

with α being the constant, β and λ coefficients and ε_t being the residuals. The appropriate lag order of the VAR model was selected by using Akaike's information criterion and Wald lag exclusion statistics.

The model is estimated based on the z-standardized data used in Lischka (2015) which are plotted against time in *Figure 14*. The original *PI* series

28 The remaining equations for *NT, NC* and *NV* of the VAR model are omitted.

remains negative throughout the observation period without strong variation with a mean of -28.24 on a scale between -100 to +100 revealing that the majority of the German population expected to spend about the same or less money on major purchases in the following twelve months (see details on the scale and measuring in the Appendix, Table 5, and the series plotted with their original scale in the Appendix, *Figure 29*). The original *FS* series is slightly negative throughout the observation period without strong variation. The original *RM* series reveals negative values except for most of 2006 peaking 32.2 in November 2006 and from July 2009 onward with positive values of 4 to 11. *PI* and *RM* are comparably low in the first two years of the observation period. *PI* reaches two subsequent bottoms in November 2002 and February 2003. Afterwards, *PI* increases to a peak in June 2006 and *RM* peaks in November 2006 whereas *PE* peaks only in May 2007. Afterwards *PI* and *RM* decline reaching their bottoms in August 2008. During the 2008/9 recession, *PI* does not drop as severely as *PE*. *RM* is above its mean before *PE* reached its bottom. After mid-2009, *PI* increases and reaches a second peak in the beginning of 2011. Hence, the developments reveal that *PI* and *RM* remain more optimistic and earlier become optimistic than *PE*. The public expects prices to increase throughout the observation period except for a short period in 2009/10 after the recession (*PT*). *PT* often moves in accordance with *RM*. When the public expects the price trend to decrease, the evaluation of the right moment to purchase increases. Thus, although—or precisely because—a deteriorating economic situation, the public assesses the recession period a good time to make major purchases.

5.1.4 Results and discussion

VAR results are summarized in Table 3 including the results of Lischka (2015) in the first column (Model 1). First, public expectations of the economic situation are partly driven by real-world indicators and news tone and volume (4a). Next, the financial situation of the household could not be effectively measured indicated by an insignificant *F* value and is by tendency influenced by previous *PE* (4b). The evaluation of price trends is affected by previous *RM* (4c). However, the estimated model also does not constitute an effective forecasting model for *PT*. The Evaluation of *RM* depends on *FS*, *PE* and *NT*, of which *PE* most strongly Granger causes *RM*

(4d). The survey question for *RM* explicitly refers to the economic situation, "In view of the general economic situation, do you think that now it is the right moment for people to make major purchases…" (European Commission 2014, 48), which explains the Granger causality of *PE*. However, again, the overall estimation is not effective. The financial situation and less strongly the evaluation of the right moment to purchase forecast purchase intention, which also strongly negatively depends on its own past (4e). In turn, purchase intention has no impact on the production index but *PT* and *PE* can forecast *EI* (4f). Thus, the public expectations of the economic development are in accordance to the future development of the economic indicator revealing that public economic assumptions are *correct*.

News tone and volume on the general economy partly influence *PE* and *RM*. Yet news has no direct but a small indirect influence on purchase intention as *PI* is Granger caused by *RM* on a 10% significance level. When news tone was negative in the past, the evaluation of the right moment improves and transmits by tendency into a greater purchase intention. In comparison, however, the expectations of the household's future financial situation has greater forecasting ability for *PI* than *RM*. These relationships with *PE, RM,* and *PI* are illustrated in *Figure 15*.

Hence, economic news tone as well as public expectations for the economy are slightly transmitted to future individual purchase intentions. However, the effect of news and *PE* on *RM* is negative. Previous research suggests a positive relation between the general economy and the intention to purchase durable goods as used in the present model, since purchases of durables can be postponed in economically insecure times. Intentions to purchase durable goods as opposed to consumer goods is an aspect of economic decision making that should be influenced by people's perception of the economic situation. However, the evaluation of the personal financial situation is not affected by real-world economic indicator, news, and only slightly by *PE*. Thus, the public may consider a downturn "announced" by economic news and manifested in economic expectations a good time to make major purchases, because people did not expect their own financial situation to be affected by the downturn.

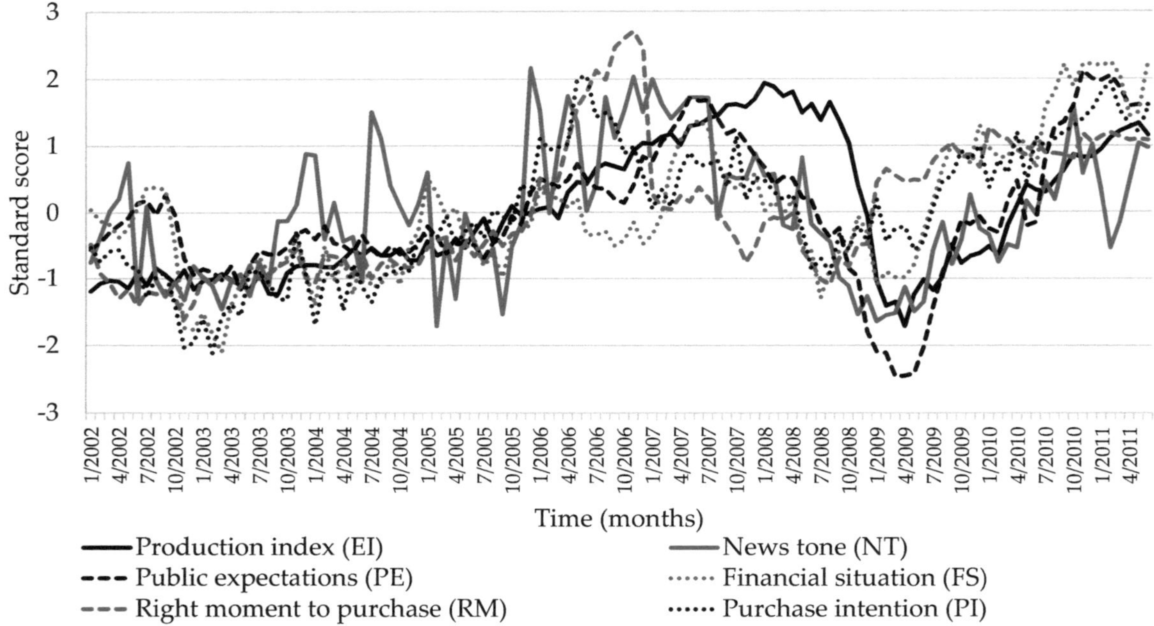

Figure 14: The production index, purchase intention, public expectations and news tone on the general economy

Notes. Observation period Jan 2002 – Jun 2011. All data are z-transformed. The German production index is published by the German Federal Statistical Office and is working day and seasonal adjusted. News tone is the monthly mean of the news on the general economy of four news outlets: *ARD Tagesschau*, *ZDF heute*, *RTL aktuell*, *BILD* (Lischka 2015, 382–85). News consonance (NC), volume (NV), and price trend (PT) are omitted for better readability.

Table 3: Relations between production index, private purchase intention, public expectations, and economic news

Dependent variable	*EI*	*PE*	*FS*	*PT*	*RM*	*PI*	*EI*
Model	1[1]	4a	4b	4c	4d	4e	4f
Δ Production index (*EI*)	*t*-3+°	*t*-1+°	n.s.	n.s.	n.s.	*t*-1+°	n.s.
	(n.a.)	(n.s.)	(n.s.)	(n.s.)	(n.s.)	(n.s.)	(n.a.)
Δ Purchase intention (*PI*)		n.s.	n.s.	n.s.	n.s.	*t*-1–***, *t*-2–*	n.s.
		(n.s.)	(n.s.)	(n.s.)	(n.s.)	(n.a.)	(n.s.)
Δ Right moment to purchase (*RM*)		n.s.	n.s.	*t*-1+**, *t*-2+°	n.s.	*t*-1+°	n.s.
		(n.s.)	(n.s.)	(5.21**)	(n.a.)	(2.947°)	(n.s.)
Δ Price trend (*PT*)		n.s.	n.s.	n.s.	n.s.	n.s.	*t*-2+**
		(n.s.)	(n.s.)	(n.a.)	(n.a.)	(n.s.)	(4.406*)
Δ Financial situation (*FS*)		n.s.	n.s.	n.s.	*t*-1+*	*t*-1+**	n.s.
		(n.s.)	(n.a.)	(n.s.)	(2.626°)	(4.767*)	(n.s.)
Δ Public expectations (*PE*)	*t*-1+**	*t*-1+°	*t*-1+°	n.s.	*t*-1–**	n.s.	*t*-1+**, *t*-2+°
	(3.842*)	(n.a.)	(n.s.)	(n.s.)	(6.18**)	(n.s.)	(8.5***)
News tone (*NT*)	n.s.	*t*-2–°	n.s.	n.s.	*t*-2–*	n.s.	n.s.
	(n.s.)	(n.s.)	(n.s.)	(n.s.)	(2.786°)	(n.s.)	(n.s.)
News tone consonance (*NC*)	n.s.	n.s.	n.s.	n.s.	n.s.	n.s.	n.s.
	(n.s.)	(n.s.)	(n.s.)	(n.s.)	(n.s.)	(n.s.)	(n.s.)
News volume (*NV*)	n.s.	*t*-1–*, *t*-2+°	n.s.	n.s.	n.s.	n.s.	n.s.
	(n.s.)	(n.s.)	(n.s.)	(n.s.)	(n.s.)	(n.s.)	(n.s.)
Constant	.012	.014	.028	-.012	.026	.015	.016
Lag structure	*t*-1, *t*-2, *t*-3	*t*-1, *t*-2	*t*-1, *t*-2	*t*-1, *t*-2	*t*-1, *t*-2	*t*-1, *t*-2	*t*-1, *t*-2
n	110	111	111	111	111	111	111
adjusted R^2	0.136	.094	-.016	.016	.052	.204	.182
F	2.060*	1.635°	.905	1.097	1.338	2.568**	2.362**
RMSE	0.210	.262	.399	.340	.314	.361	.202
Durbin–Watson *d* statistic	1.959	2.084	2.084	2.084	2.084	2.084	2.084
LM test (chi^2)	46.347**	79.814	79.814	79.814	79.814	79.814	79.814

Notes. Observation period January 2002 – June 2011. 1 Taken from Lischka (2015, 389, Table 3, column 1). Cells contain the lags and signs of significant VAR coefficients with Granger causality F value in parentheses. For Granger causality, the null hypotheses that the coefficients on all the lags of an endogenous variable are jointly zero is tested. n.s.: not significant, °: significant on 10% level, *: significant on 5% level, **: significant on 1% level, ***: significant on .1% level. EI for general economy is the production index. PE question for general economy, "How do you expect the general economic situation in this country to develop over the next 12 months?" (European Commission 2014, 48). Lagrange-multiplier (LM) tests (H0: no autocorrelation at lag order) are performed and test values of the highest lag are reported.

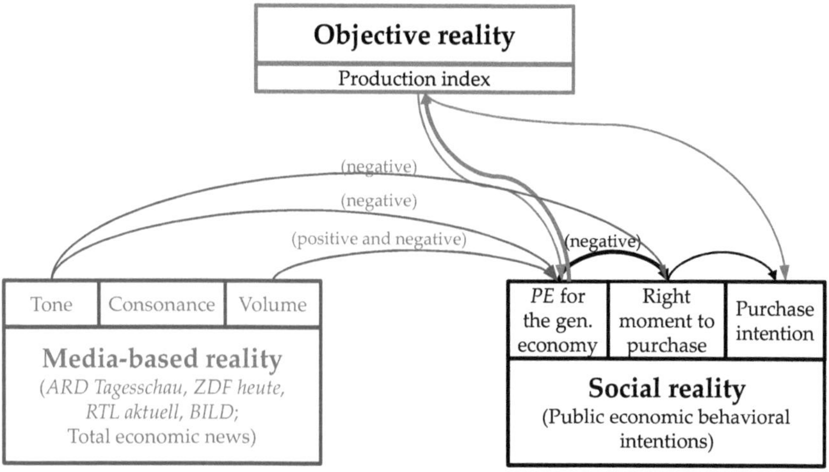

Figure 15: Main influences on purchase intention of the public

Notes. Stronger influences are indicated with thicker arrows. If not stated differently, arrows indicate positive effects.

The lack of a direct relationship between *PE* and *PI* may additionally be caused by a difference in specificity—by the fact that *individual* purchase intentions are on a different dimension from the *national* general economy. To find relationships between attitudes and behavior, the two are required to correspond on a matter at hand. As stated by Mutz (1992), sociotropic and egocentric evaluations are not necessarily in a close relationship. Hence, *national*, i.e., sociotropic sentiment and *individual*, i.e., egocentric behavior are not in correspondence.

According to Katona (1957; 1974), as discussed in Section 5.1.1, purchase behavior depends on (1) the purchaser's personal financial situation, (2) the general economic outlook, and (3) the ability to buy. The model estimated here includes the general economic outlook and the personal financial situation but omits the ability to buy, e.g. measured by income. Therefore, the model quality is low for the financial situation (4b).

To sum up, news tone and volume as well as public economic expectations are in an indirect, negative relationship with purchase intention mediated by the evaluation of the right moment to purchase. Thus, news deliver signals for expectations for the economic situation and the evaluation of a good time to make purchases and thus indirectly affects consumption behavior. This negative indirect effect is in contrast to previous research, because previous research assumes that people's financial situation and ability to buy decreases in downturns. But since the personal financial situation is not considered to be affected in a downturn, a more pessimistic outlook on the general economy rather improves purchase intention. The public correctly *assumes* the aggregate economic situation—and the economic sentiment of the public *indirectly negatively guides* economic behavior.

5.2 Corporate economic behavior: Advertising expenditures

This section briefly revises the literature on the influence of public economic sentiment, consumption behavior and economic news on corporate investment decisions, especially advertising expenditures (Section 5.2.1). The role of economic expectations in economic decision making and the economy is briefly explained in Lischka and Siegert (2013, 175). Advertising budgeting processes are described in Lischka, Kienzler, and Mellmann (2014). An additional empirical analysis on the temporal relationship between economic news and advertising expenditures is presented in Sections 5.2.2 and 5.2.3.

5.2.1 The influence of economic news and private economic sentiment on advertising expenditures

More recently, scholars have used consumer confidence to forecast real-world economic indicators other than consumption. Heim (2009) argues that consumer confidence affects corporate investments since businesses try to detect market changes and consumer confidence affects consumer spending. However, the consumer confidence index used had no additional forecasting ability for an investment model unless other variables (capacity utilization, business profitability, Dow Jones Composite Index, Real Prime Interest Rate) were included as control variables. A consumer *expectations* index that was used had additional forecasting ability for the investment model estimated. Hence, investment might be at least weakly related to consumer expectations (Heim 2009, 17). Likewise, Dailami and

Masson (2009) argue that consumer and investor confidence are related. Adrangi and Macri (2011) state that results of consumer confidence surveys are reported in economic news and therefore play an important role for business decision making. The role of news is therefore twofold. First, economic news may affect the economic expectations of the public, which may in turn affect consumption behavior. Second, news informs the corporate decision maker about consumer sentiment and provides hints for consumer behavior. According to Gunther and Storey (2003), news affects assumptions through an influence of presumed influence. That is, beliefs about others' beliefs and behavior affect an actor's behavior as described by Jepperson (2002, 232), "the basic 'myths' of society operate primarily by establishing beliefs about what others think and expectations about how others will 'behave'." Such a reality myth or presumption can explain why economic news potentially affects corporate decision makers' behavior.

Yet advertising attempts to create demand and generate sales, which is suggested by the activist view (Bagwell 2001; Galbraith 1967; Jones 2007).[29] However, if sales depend on sentiments on the economy, advertising and marketing activities compete with these sentiments. At the same time, advertising activities are often planned based on present or past sales or sales expectations (see the overview in Kienzler and Lischka 2015, Table 2.2 or Lischka, Kienzler, and Mellmann 2014, 13, Table 1). Lischka, Kienzler, and Mellmann (2014) have shown that past sales are especially capable of advertising expenditures in the automobile industry, and argue that sales expectations influence future advertising budgets in the drinks, textiles and clothing industries as well as the shoes and leather goods industries. The more car sales where realized in the previous year, the more advertising expenditures are budgeted today. The authors argue that the purchase of durable goods is highly postponable compared with the purchase of nondurable goods (see discussion in Lischka, Kienzler, and Mellmann 2014, 34–35). Durable goods purchases and especially car purchases depend on income and income expectations and therefore on the economic situation. Even though the share of news concerned with consumer sentiment is very low (2 – 7% of economic news in the major German news outlets [see Lischka 2014a, 15, Table 2]) and although Section 5.1 showed

29 Although advertising activities might not always aim directly at sales effects or might fail to do so. Advertising expenditures are only one factor for advertising effectiveness as discussed in Lischka, Kienzler, and Mellmann (2014, 40).

that private purchase intention is barely affected by economic sentiment, business decision makers might presume news effects on the public as shown in Lischka and Siegert (2013) for economic experts.

Hence, if corporate decision makers presume that economic news guides purchase behavior and adapt advertising expenditures accordingly, economic news can forecast advertising expenditures.

5.2.2 Data and measurement

In Lischka, Kienzler, and Mellmann (2014), results reveal that future sales expectations guide advertising expenditures in the drinks, textiles and clothing as well as shoes and leather goods industries. For the present analysis, the VAR model estimated in Lischka, Kienzler, and Mellmann (2014) is extended with the economic news tone of *ARD Tagesschau* and *ZDF heute* as used in Lischka and Siegert (2013).

Figure 16 plots advertising expenditures and economic news tone against time. The average movement of the time series is quite similar. Advertising expenditures decrease during the first observed year and remain on average until about 2005 when an increase starts reaching the top in the end of 2006/2007. Advertising expenditures for food and drinks as well as textiles and clothing decrease from 2007 throughout 2008 whereas advertising expenditures for shoes and leather goods and automobile remain stable and decrease only in the beginning of 2009.

Due to the short observation period of 32 quarters, thrifty VAR models are estimated allowing two lags of advertising expenditures (*AE*) and news tone (*NT*) to influence advertising expenditures at time *t*. The GDP (*GDP*) is included to control effects of the current state of the economy. The VAR model[30] has the form

(5a) $\Delta AE_t = \alpha_1 + \beta_1 \Delta AE_{t-n} + \lambda_1 NT_{ARD,t-n} + \lambda_2 NT_{ZDF,t-n} + \gamma_1 \Delta GDP_t + \varepsilon_t$

with α being the constant, β, λ and γ coefficients and ε_t being the residuals. Since the number of observations is low and only few lags can be included in order not to excess the VAR model, results have to be interpreted with caution.

30 Since only to explain advertising expenditures (*AE*) is of interest, the remaining equations of the VAR model are omitted.

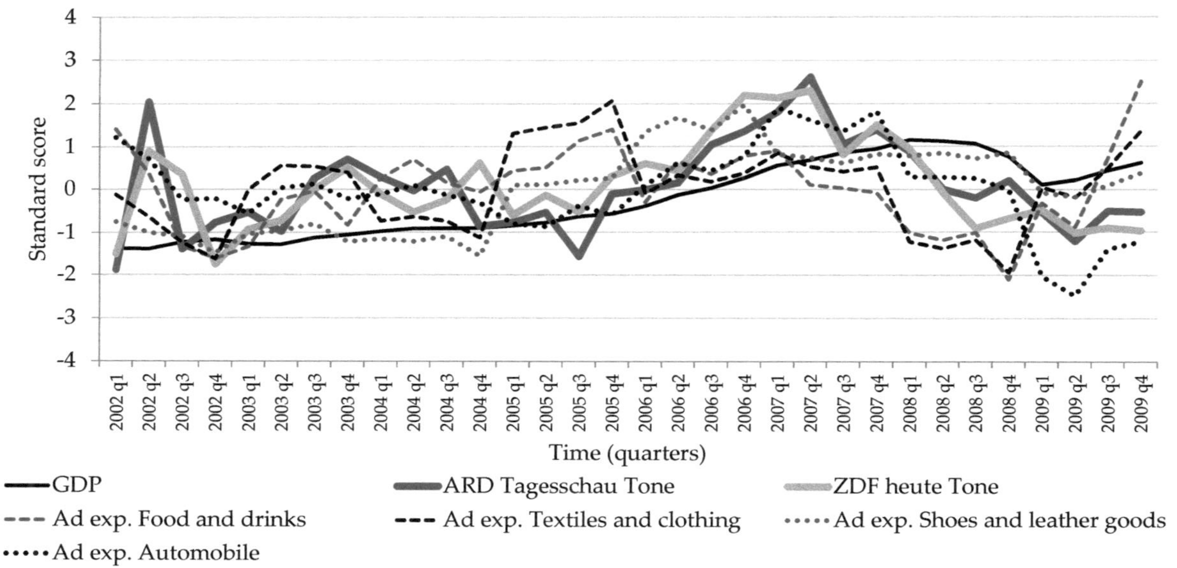

Figure 16: The GDP, advertising expenditures per industry and public-service economic news tone

Notes. Advertising expenditures stem from Nielsen Media Research, as published in *Media Perspektiven* (gross advertising expenditures in Germany) and are seasonally corrected. News tone is the quarterly mean of the *total* economic news per outlet.

5.2.3 Results and discussion

Results in Table 4 reveal that the coefficients in all models have to be interpreted with caution since either the *F* value is insignificant or the LM value is significant. Thus, the VAR results have only preliminary character.

Changes in food and drinks advertising expenditures strongly vary based on expenditures of the previous quarter. If expenditures increased in the previous quarter, they decrease in the current quarter, and vice versa (indicated by *t*-1–**). Since no other coefficients have a significant influence, this relation can explain about 60% of the variance in current advertising expenditures. However, the LM test indicates further information within the residuals. Thus, the VAR model used for estimating food and drinks advertising expenditures is not effective enough. The negative relation of advertising expenditures with previous advertising expenditures is found for all industries. Thus, advertising expenditures increase and decrease from quarter to quarter beyond seasonal effects.

Economic news tone of *ARD Tagesschau* and *ZDF heute* have a lagged negative influence on shoes and leather goods as well as automobile advertising expenditures. The coefficients of one past quarter (*t*-1) reveal that the more negative news tone, the more advertising budget will be spent in the next quarter. And, vice versa, the more positive news tone, the less advertising budget will be spent. In addition, advertising expenditures of the automobile industry tends to be positively influenced by the current state of the economy (*GDP*). That is, the more positive the general economic development, the more advertising is spent in the current quarter, indicating a pro-cyclical advertising strategy. The main influences are graphically displayed in *Figure 17*.

A negative news-advertising relationship can be interpreted as increasing advertising activities to compensate negative news tone. This reaction to economic news is justifiable with future-oriented, anti-cyclical budgeting strategies. Future-oriented advertising budgeting takes assumed sales into account. If advertisers expect a decline in sales in the future—which may be indicated by negative economic news—they can either set their advertising budget pro- or anti-cyclically to their sales expectations (see Lischka, Kienzler, and Mellmann 2014, 33–34 for pro- and anti-cyclical as well as past-, present-, or future-oriented advertising budgeting). A pro-cyclical reaction is a decrease and an anti-cyclical reaction an increase in advertising budget when a decline in sales is expected.

Table 4: Influence of public-service economic news tone on advertising expenditures per industry

	Advertising expenditures per industry			
Dependent variable:	Food and drinks	Textiles and clothing	Shoes and leather goods	Automobile
Δ Past of dependent variable	*t*-1–**	*t*-1–°	*t*-1–°	*t*-1–**
NT ARD Tagesschau	n.s.	*t*-1–°	*t*-1–*	*t*-1–°
NT ZDF heute	n.s.	n.s.	*t*-1–*	n.s.
Δ *GDP t*	n.s.	n.s.	n.s.	*t*+°
Constant	.431	.073	.353	–.072
Lag structure	*t*-1, *t*-2	*t*-1, *t*-2	*t*-1	*t*-1, *t*-2
n	29	29	30	29
adjusted R^2	0.633	0.181	0.075	0.238
F	7.402***	1.664	2.352°	2.013
RMSE	1.144	.930	.356	.681
Durbin–Watson *d*–statistic	1.927	1.782	1.855	1.950
LM test (*chi*²)	39.997***	9.739	8.192	10.253

Notes. Cells contain the lags and signs of significant VAR coefficients. n.s.: not significant, °: significant on 10% level, *: significant on 5% level, **: significant on 1% level. Time horizon 2002 Q1 – 2009 Q4. 1 Lagrange-multiplier (LM) tests (H0: no autocorrelation at lag order) are performed and test values of the highest lag (t – 2) are reported.

When the available income decreases for households, it is especially the purchase of durable goods that can be postponed (see discussion in Lischka, Kienzler, and Mellmann 2014, 34–35). In order to actively manage consumer demand through marketing activities as early suggested by Galbraith (1967), an immediate increase in the following quarter's advertising budget may balance out *presumed* negative effects of news tone on public purchase behavior. This is in line with the activist view that advertising expenditures will increase sales by influencing consumers' inter-temporal preferences (Bagwell 2001; Jones 2007).

However, a long-term budgeting strategy may reveal pro-cyclical tendencies for advertising budgeting, as suggested by the positive forecasting tendency of GDP for automobile advertising expenditures. As companies realize a decrease in revenue, their available budget for advertising (and other) expenditures decreases. This is in line with the deterministic view stating that "whenever manufacturers realize more revenues from sales, they tend to spend more on advertising" (Hsu et al. 2002, 187), implying past-oriented advertising budgeting. An advertising cutback due to recessions and a resulting decrease in advertising income by media companies is verified in previous research (Kienzler and Lischka 2013; Picard

2001; van der Wurff, Bakker, and Picard 2008). As they are the dominant contributor to media companies, media markets struggle as a result (Gustafsson 2006; Siegert et al. 2012; van der Wurff, Bakker, and Picard 2008).

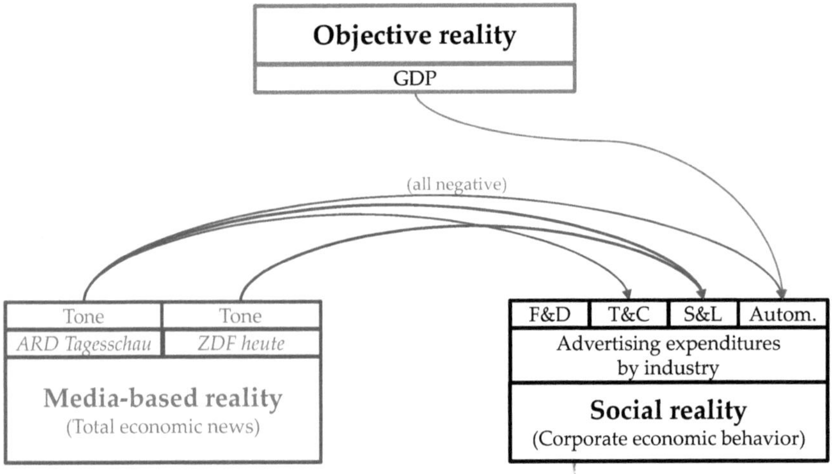

Figure 17: Main influences on advertising expenditures per industry

Notes. If not stated differently, arrows indicate positive effects. Due to *F* or LM test values of the VAR models, all relations are provisional and have to be interpreted with caution. F&D = Food and drinks, T&C = Textiles and clothing, S&L = Shoes and leather goods, Autom. = Automobile.

Hence, there is some evidence that economic news might influence advertising expenditures on an industry level beyond the effects of the general economic situation, due to presumed news effects on public purchase behavior. Results suggest a connection between public and corporate economic expectations as suggested by previous studies (Adrangi and Macri 2011; Dailami and Masson 2009). To gain a clearer picture, a richer model based on a longer observation period would be beneficial. Further variables on the aggregate economy and industry level that influence advertising decision making should be included.

5.3 Interim summary and conclusions

Tracing the relation between social and objective economic realities including economic behavior as illustrated in *Figure 1* (path C), the following interim conclusion can be drawn from the discussion of this study's results against the theoretical background and previous research.

C. The public makes correct assumptions about the future economic situation and unemployment development. However, public economic expectations are not in a direct relation with intentional economic behavior on an aggregate level, but the relation is mediated by the judgment whether it is a good time to purchase. A lack of correspondence between *individual* purchase intention and *national* economic expectations as well as the people's assessment that their financial situation is not affected in a downturn can be held responsible for the absent direct relation. Since the personal financial situation is not considered to be affected in a downturn, more pessimistic news and expectations on the general economy improves the judgment of a good time to purchase, which, in turn, improves purchase intention.

    Although economic experts may not expect that corporate investments rely on general economic news (see Section 4.2), advertising expenditures as a subcategory of corporate investments can be partly explained by economic news tone. Similar to economic experts presuming that public economic decisions are in line with economic news (Section 4.2), advertising budgeting decisions considering future sales expectations may take economic news tone into account. Hence, corporate advertising decision makers may presume that private consumption behavior is geared by economic news.

    Hence, although "...the car dealers (...) want all stories involving auto sales to have a rosy outlook, and they whine about negative economic stories, even if they're on a national level from AP" (Soley and Craig 1992, 7), people may not stop buying cars because of bad economic news or pessimistic national economic expectations.

6 Overall summary and conclusions

This study measures the relations between objective reality, media-based reality, and social reality including behavior for the economy in aggregate. Therefore, it broadens the classical mass communication research focus on the relationship between objective and media reality or the relationship between media and social reality, but focuses on the whole cycle between objective, media-based, and social realities. This entails going beyond the question of whether economic news can influence people's agendas and asking whether news can also influence people's economic behavior. Hence, economic sentiment is not only regarded as a dependent but also as an independent variable. In terms of the news-sentiment-behavior relationship, private and corporate decision makers are considered.

The final section summarizes the theoretical approach (6.1), critically discusses the limitations of the analysis as well as suggesting areas for further research (6.2), and draws conclusions for society, economic journalism, and media financing (6.3).

6.1 Theoretical approach

This book develops a theoretical model that dynamically connects real-world economic indicators, economic news and economic sentiment over time. Based on Bonfadelli's (2004, 237) triangular agenda-setting model, agenda building and news making, first- and second-level agenda setting, bounded rationality, the persuasive press inference (Gunther 1998, 486) and the influence of presumed influence (Gunther and Storey 2003) as well as the role of economic sentiment for economic behavior are discussed. Micro foundations (Coleman 1986; 1990) combining attitudinal and behavioral aspects and the research on collective effects and temporal relations (Rössler 1997) are complemented. The micro level of Coleman's macro-micro-macro model is crucial to implement economic behavior into the triangular agenda-setting model.

Based on this theoretical outline, the literature is reviewed for the relation between objective and media-based realities, the media and the social as well as the social and the objective realities. Regarding the relation between the objective and the media realities, i.e., agenda building, the journalists' inability to provide a reproduction of the real world (Weischenberg 1994, 427) and the role of organizational influences on news making are examined. Concerning the relation between the media and the social realities, public agenda setting, media dependency (Ball-Rokeach and DeFleur 1976), the obtrusiveness of economic topics and the obtrusive contingency hypothesis (Blood 1981; Zucker 1978) as well as the sociotropic character of economic sentiments (Hagen May 27, 2004; Mutz 1992) are discussed. For the expert's agenda setting, the effect of presumed influence (Gunther and Storey 2003) as a third-person effect (Davison 1983) is considered. To explain the relation between social and objective realities, sentiment is discussed as intermediary variable between economic information and public as well as corporate economic behavior according to Katona (1957). For corporate economic behavior, the role of expected public behavior is explored on the level of corporate advertising budgeting and private consumption behavior (Kienzler and Lischka 2015; Jepperson 2002).

The theoretical considerations expect that economic news aligns with real-world developments but cannot copy them. Subsequently, economic news on national issues should have only a limited ability to forecast public economic sentiment and even less ability to forecast the sentiment of economic experts due to the obtrusiveness of the topic and low media dependency but good accessibility of real-world cues. Yet both a higher consonance of news coverage and a recession period should enhance news effects. Theory and previous research leads to the expectation that economic sentiment will guide economic behavior that adds up to real-world economic indicators. Hence, when referring to the relations between the realities as lined out in *Figure 1,* theory and previous research suggest that the objective-media and media-social relationships may be weak whereas the sentiment-behavior relationship as part of the social-objective relation should be stronger.

6.2 Limitations and further research

The analysis is based on secondary data from different sources reflecting the population or experts, aggregate national or industry level. A major limitation is related to the use of secondary data, which is the lack of a connection on the micro level of the individual or the company. For example, the actual news use by surveyed individuals remains unknown. A recent research project by Kalogeropoulos et al. (2015) avoid this limitation by conducting a panel study collecting data on media use, economic knowledge and perceptions (see also van Dalen et al. 05.02.2015). The drawback is the high number of panel waves that would be necessary for VAR estimations. Hence, an ideal solution for research would be the inclusion of questions on media use and economic news perception to monthly or quarterly conducted expert, business or consumer climate surveys.

While dynamics over time were estimated in the present study, dynamics between macro and micro level, i.e., cross-level dynamics (Scheufele 2008, 356), remain uncovered. Thus, there is a danger of ecological fallacy when measuring on an aggregate level and concluding on processes on the micro level. The probability of making ecological fallacies, shortcomings due to secondary data used, and limitations of VAR estimations are discussed in the following.

The goal of the news outlet selection was to cover the most important news outlets in terms of reach in Germany, to cover an average news portfolio, as well as to represent Germany's pluralistic media system. Thus, the news outlet selection covers general news aiming at an economically lay audience. This news outlet selection allows the analysis of collective agenda-setting effects for the public. The measures of the media reality match the news use of the population but insufficiently the news use of experts or corporate decision makers. In addition, the population is a subset of the national level of the objective reality. Hence, the aggregation levels are not completely equal.

The analysis of collective media effects on the social reality does not require a micro level connection—as long as the social structure and the level of aggregation is similar between the samples (Hagen 2005, 26–27) and the level of news consonance within and across news outlets is sufficiently high, which is relevant for follow-up conversation (Maurer 2004; Wanta 1997). Previous research affirms that "news media collectively can exert considerable agenda-setting influence over their audiences," whereas differences in agenda-setting effects related to media channels or media types are not found (Strömbäck and Kiousis 2010, 289). Data on economic news are based on the coding of the total economic news of each investigated news show and on the first three pages of the investigated tabloid newspaper. The consonance of the news tone for each news outlet and over all selected news outlets is taken into account in the analyses.

Still, quality newspapers such as the *Frankfurter Allgemeine Zeitung* or the *Süddeutsche Zeitung* that obtain a minor reach compared with the selected news outlets but may serve as leading media outlets and therefore set the intermedia agenda (Jarren and Vogel 2009; Mast 2012, 211–94; Noelle-Neumann and Mathes 1987). However, also the *ARD Tagesschau* news serves as a leading media outlet and guides other news outlets (Weischenberg, Löffelholz, and Scholl 1994). Furthermore, news outlets specified to economic and business news aiming at an economically professional audience such as the *Handelsblatt* or *ManagerMagazin* were not included. Both news types may especially be valuable when estimating intermedia agenda setting. The lack of further news outlets could involve two limitations. First, the total economic news consonance over various types of news outlets cannot be estimated. Second, if news tone of quality newspapers differs considerably from the news tone of the selected news outlets in the present study, a lack of relationships between economic news and public sentiment may be attributed to differences in sentiment that transmits in follow-up conversations. The quality newspapers mentioned are read by better educated people who may be early recognizers or opinion leaders. Their economic sentiments are more likely to be accepted in follow-up conversations by others. However, since such print news outlets serve as key media and set the intermedia agenda, consonant economic news between them and the selected news outlets in the present study can be expected (Noelle-Neumann and Mathes 1987, see also e.g., Eilders 2002 on the degree of consonance in German quality newspapers; Degenhard 2011 concerning the synchronal behavior of German newspapers and conformity of the media system). Further, a high similarity in issue salience among German TV news and a close relationship between the agenda of early recognizers and German TV evening news agenda was revealed by previous research (Brosius and Weimann 1996). Therefore, the news can be considered consonant across news outlets in Germany and the present study should not suffer too much from an exclusion of other news media.

In addition, online news content was not part of the current study. While Mast (2012) shows that online news were no major source of economic information compared to traditional media for the German public and corporate decision makers in a 2010/11 survey, Schifferes and Coulter (2013) reveal that the traffic of the business section of the *BBC News* website notably increased during the global financial crisis. Shehata and Strömbäck (2013) demonstrate decreasing agenda-setting effects of traditional news media when online news outlets are increasingly used. If news characteristics differ between traditional and online news, the present study may underestimate agenda-setting effects due to a missing analysis of online news sources.

The coding of news content used in the present study reveals the media-based reality of traditional, general news outlets. Moreover, this study analyzed news tone consonance for broad and rather obtrusive economic news topics. Measuring news tone consonance on a narrower and less obtrusive economic issue may reveal an interaction effect of consonance for second-level agenda setting. But it still cannot give evidence on what may turn out to be the *perceived* news tone as used for example in Starr (2012). Both the perceived news tone and the tone of follow-up conversations are important to understanding agenda-setting processes and should be considered in future research. For example, to analyze tweets or comments on online news on the economy could reveal how the public interprets journalistic interpretation and which news tone more likely transfers to follow-up conversations—although users of social networks are less likely to address economic issues (Neuman et al. 2014, 210).

To study objective reality, the GDP, the production index and the unemployment rate were selected on aggregate level. The former two indicators relate to the current state of the economy, the latter one is a following indicator of the economy. The GDP is based on the market value of the final goods of all industries within a nation (production approach) and includes corporate investments, private consumption and government spending (expenditure approach). Unemployment numbers result from in- or decreasing productivity. The lagging characteristic of unemployment can explain that the production index as current indicator of the economy better forecasts public expectations on national unemployment.

For economic sentiment, this book focuses on expectations for the development of the general economy and unemployment based on a quota sample of the German population, because forward-looking expectations are assumed to be more relevant for future economic behavior than the evaluation of the current state of the economy or unemployment.

Consumer behavior was measured by purchase intention, which is not identical with *performed* purchase behavior. According to Ajzen (1985, 29, italic in original), "Strictly speaking, intentions can only be expected to predict a person's *attempt* to perform a behavior, not necessarily its actual performance." Intentions are found to have a moderate relationship with performed behavior in meta studies (mean $r = .49$ according to Sheppard, Jon Hartwick, and Warshaw 1988; accounting for 27% of variance in behavior according to Armitage and Conner 2001). Because a large part of human behavior is not fully volitionally controlled by the acting individual due to lacking motivations, cognitive capabilities and also depends on the attitude toward the behavior or subjective norms (Armitage and Conner 2001), purchase intention can differ from actual performed purchase behavior. In order to complete the causal path from news sentiment and attitudinal sentiment to purchase behavior, indicators of performed behavior, i.e., consumption figures, should be added in future research.

For advertising expenditures, aggregation at an industry level might balance out differences in advertising budgeting decision making between companies *within* an industry. Collective behavior on a company level are questionable since many practices for and influences on advertising budgeting exist. From the analysis of news, sales and advertising, conclusions on expenditures on an industry level can only be made based on the average behavior of an industry but not on the behavior of the companies within each industry. Here, a danger of ecological fallacy exists when concluding on the decision making of *one* company.

This book's analysis goes beyond the estimation of simultaneous relations but explores truly dynamic relations by estimating VAR models. VAR models take dynamic leading and lagging relations between the objects of investigation into account. VAR analysis and the concept of Granger causality enable concluding on preceding or subsequent relationships. The VAR coefficient reveals a linear relationship between a variable X at time $t - n$ on Y at time t (Sims 1980). It also shows how strongly Y depends on its own past. Granger causality exposes whether a variable Y at time t can be significantly better forecast by using the past of another variable X instead of its own past alone (Granger 1969). If so, X Granger causes Y. However, to infer genuine causality requires profound theoretical arguments. In addition, the analysis reveals temporal leading or lagging Granger causal relationships but does not consider simultaneous relationships. This means that, although leading or lagging relations may not be found, simultaneous connections may exist.

This book estimates dynamic relations between objective, media, and social realities for 32 (economic news and advertising), 38 (economic news and experts' sentiments), 76 (advertising and sales) and 114 (economic indicators, economic news, and public sentiment) time intervals. On the one hand, VAR modeling on as few as 32 and 38 cases comprises very small samples. On the other hand, fewer cases represent a higher degree of temporal aggregation (quarters instead of months) and therefore one quarter includes the temporal aggregated information of three months. Further, all models were estimated using a small-sample degrees-of-freedom adjustment when estimating the error variance-covariance matrix and report small-sample t and F statistics.

The observation periods include the dotcom crisis in 2000, a slight recession in 2003/4, the financial crises following the subprime crisis from 2007 onwards, and a severe recession in 2008/9 in Germany followed by the Euro crisis (see e.g. Schirwitz 2009; Statistisches Bundesamt 2012; Räth 2009 for definitions of recession periods in Germany). Therefore, results enable statements on the relations in upturn and recession periods as well as in an international crisis as suggested by previous research on effects of economic news (Blood and Phillips 1995).

6.3 Final discussion and conclusions

The present results reveal that temporal relations between the three realities are weak. Small forecasting abilities between the objective and media-based realities as well between as media and social realities could be expected and were found. But the relationship between sentiment and behavior was expected to be stronger than found in this study's results. Yet the present results can enhance previous research. Effects of news on public behavior depend on the extent to which they are affected by a situation in their personal life, whereas news effects on corporate actors depend on assumed behavior of customers.

Figure 18 provides a simplified overview of the relations between objective, media-based and social realities. Most temporal relations between objective, media, and social realities vary over time according to the economic situation. The 2008/9 recession constitutes an especially important period, causing changes to occur in the media-based reality among news outlets and affecting social reality as well.

In the following, the main results are summarized and conclusions are given on each relationship.

A. Economic news is no copy of the real-world aggregate economy. News issues and their tone, consonance and volume on the same topic are diverse and therefore more volatile than aggregate economic indicators. Yet economic news reflects the aggregate reality when the topic is less elusive and complex or the economic situation is critical. Real-world employment-related events that become part of the news are more closely related to aggregate unemployment numbers, while events that are selected for news on the general economy seems to fluctuate strongly compared with the general state of the economy—especially during stable economic periods. The most stable relationship revealed between objective and news-based realities is that journalistic news interpretation becomes more consonant following economic downturns and increased unemployment, and less consonant after positive changes. Hence, social mechanisms of reference (Weischenberg 1994) and therefore second-level agenda building, i.e., real-world influences on news tone, depend on the elusiveness of a topic and on the negative significance of an event.

   News tone, consonance, and volume differ in level among the private news outlets and between the private and public service news outlets considered in this book, especially during the financial crisis period. These differences can be ascribed to organizational influences on news making, as suggested by Reinemann (2007) and Jäckel (2007). Yet, the trend over time is similar for private and public service news outlets. Thus, norms, structures, and actors on the meso level of the profession's and news company's formal and informal rules and conventions (Altmeppen 2006, 119) affect differences in the *level* of news characteristics but not changes in the *trend*. Trend changes are stimulated by real-world events that lead to changes in journalistic working modes (Scheufele 2003).

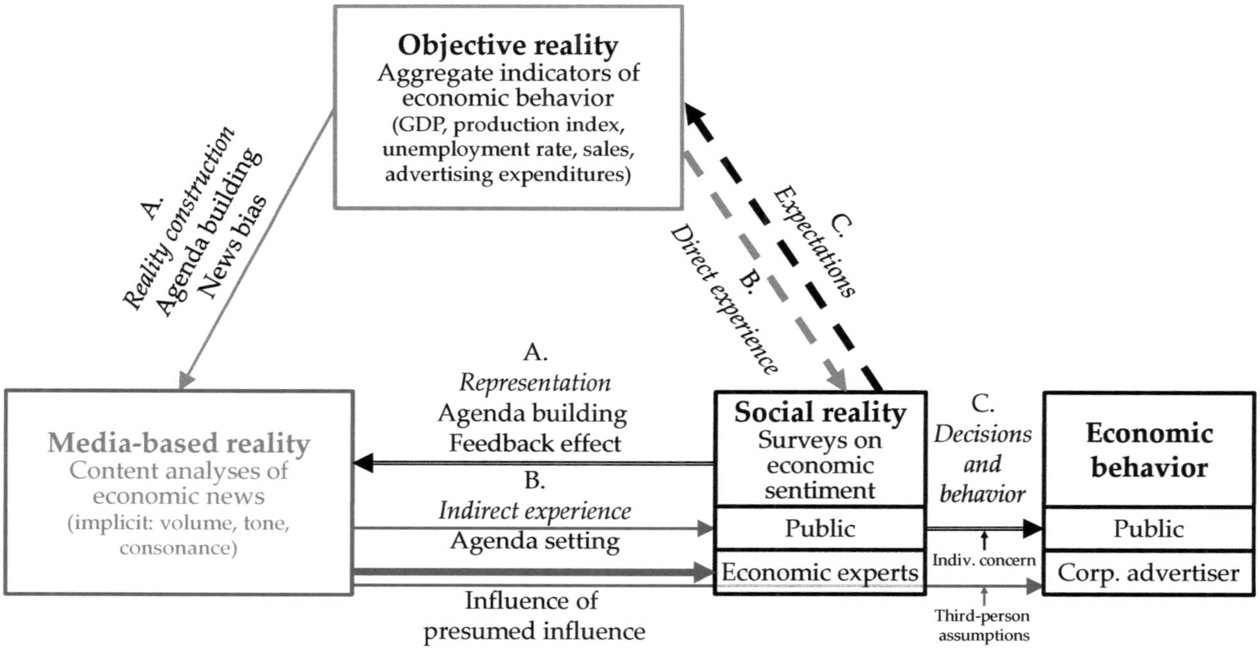

Figure 18: Empirical relations between objective, media-based, and social economic realities

Source: Compiled by the author based on Bonfadelli (2004, 237).

Notes. Stronger influences are indicated with thicker arrows. Double-lined arrows represent theoretical but no empirical confirmed direct relations.

B. The public economic sentiment depends more strongly on real-world cues than on economic news. The lack of agenda setting effects may be caused by habituated *information inertia*. Public economic expectations strongly depend on their own past, i.e., are strongly autoregressive. People's own experience is more likely than the news to be a source of tips on the general economic situation and unemployment. As suggested by Haller and Norpoth (1997, 573), the economy is a "doorstep issue" that is directly accessible in people's daily lives. Public expectations are not as volatile in their development as is news coverage, over time. Although this book focuses on sociotropic perceptions which are said to depend rather strongly on news (Hagen May 27, 2004; Mutz 1992), national economic news topics can be considered obtrusive (Demers et al. 1989; Ju 2008) and more dependent on real-world experiences according to the obtrusive contingency hypothesis (Blood 1981; Zucker 1978). Results reveal that real-world economic indicators forecast public sociotropic expectations better and more consistently, supporting the obtrusive contingency hypothesis. Before 2007, the public is barely influenced by economic news. From 2007 onwards or during the 2008/9 recession, news tone and volume can partly forecast public sociotropic economic expectations. Hence, the news may indicate whether an economic situation should be perceived as a social *problem,* as suggested by Mutz (1992). News effects on the public can be interpreted to be in line with the persuasive press inference (Gunther 1998).

The relation between news and social reality estimated with aggregate indicators potentially measures collective media effects and is supposed to depend on news consonance (Hagen 2005, 30; Maurer 2004, 410). However, news consonance does not increase news tone effects but news volume sometimes does. Instead, a decline in news consonance tends to lead to more positive economic sentiment of the public. The public might interpret less consonant news tone on the same topic as a positive sign. Yet the increase of news volume leads to stronger collective news tone effects on economic expectations. Doms and Morin (2004) state that consumers update their economic expectations more frequently during periods of high news coverage, which is the case during recessions. News volume effects can also be explained with research revealing that message repetition is related to increased statement credibility (Koch and Zerback 2013). However, simply "more" instead of a "more of the same tone" is sufficient to increase second-level agenda-setting effects.

From 2007 onward, the public relies more than experts on the news for developing their sentiment on the general economy. The experts' economic evaluation of the current state of the economy can be weakly forecast through news tone—but not their expectations. However, interestingly, economic experts rely on economic news when they evaluate current and future private consumption. This result can be interpreted as a presumption of experts that the public adjusts its consumption behavior to economic news. This is in line with the third-person effect of the presumed influence of news on a heterogeneous group of people (Gunther and Storey 2003).

In terms of societal implications, economic news does not have the power to shift public economic expectations without the support of real-world experiences. But especially increasing news volume in insecure times alarms people about economic recessions and supports the notion of a national problem.

C. Although the public makes correct assumptions about developments in the economy and unemployment, economic news or expectations does not directly affect economic behavior of the public, as measured by the intention to purchase major durable goods. Instead, news tone and volume as well as public economic expectations are in an indirect, negative relationship with purchase intention that is mediated by the judgment whether it is the right moment to purchase. Since the personal financial situation is not considered to be affected in a downturn, a more pessimistic outlook on the general economy rather improves purchase intention. The individual's personal financial situation and the ability to buy are non-sociotropic but egocentric measures (Mutz 1992) and better correspond to the individual intention to purchase, indicated by a strong forecasting ability of the household's financial situation. Thus, results of this analysis are in line with previous research revealing that news barely exerts an influence on such egocentric evaluations (Hagen May 27, 2004; Mutz 1992).

Corporate advertising expenditures can partly be forecast by economic news tone. Although bad economic news does not cause a decrease in private purchase intention, bad news may lead to an increase in corporate advertising expenditures. Hence, corporate decision makers may expect that news influences the economic behavior of the public which would also be in line with the influence of presumed influence (Gunther and Storey 2003). In fact, the actual economic news effect is less strong than expected by third parties, which explains why "...the car dealers (...) want all stories involving auto sales to have a rosy outlook, and they whine about negative economic stories, even if they're on a national level from AP" (Soley and Craig 1992, 7). Therefore, economic news not only indicates consumer confidence by reporting the results of consumer surveys (Adrangi and Macri 2011) but delivers implicit signals on consumer confidence through economic news tone. An increase in advertising activities may balance out the presumed effects of bad news and secure consumption, which is in line with the idea of actively managing consumer demand with marketing activities (Galbraith 1967; Katona 1974). On the other hand, a recession that settles into negative economic news for the long term is linked to a deteriorating ability of the public to purchase, which may not be balanced out with higher advertising expenditures. Also, decreasing purchase ability and therefore decreasing sales reduce available budgets in companies, which leads to decreasing advertising expenditures. This is in line with the deterministic view stating that "whenever manufacturers realize more revenues from sales, they tend to spend more on advertising" (Hsu et al. 2002, 187). If advertisers set their media budgets according to economic news, constantly long-term negative economic news related to a recession leads to a decrease in advertising income for media companies, as found by previous research (Picard 2001; van der Wurff, Bakker, and Picard 2008). On the other hand, short-term negative news may lead to an increase in advertising budgets, as suggested by the present results.

Overall, economic news is partly responsible for setting the public economic sentiment—and can partly indirectly influence the economic behavior of the public. But this latter influence is negative, i.e., negative news indirectly increases purchase intention because the public then thinks a downturn is a good time for major purchases. Hence, news that is too pessimistic cannot cause a decrease in consumption or even a recession—at least as long as the personal financial situation is not affected. Not only the strength of the recession but also the economic situation before a recession may determine whether economic behavior is linked to economic expectations or economic news. Of course, citizens who make well-informed economic decisions are essential to an economy (Stiglitz 2011, 23). However, news is only one source of economic information among many. Since people perceive economic indicators every day, the news media play a fairly unimportant role in setting national economic expectations and an even minor role in determining individual economic purchase behavior. In contrast, if experts or corporate agents develop expectations of the economic behavior of heterogeneous "others," economic news does play a role. That is, economic behavior of the public is presumed through implicit news cues and to some degree translates "into entrepreneurial decisions, particularly investments" (Noelle-Neumann 1987, 292). However, the presumption of the effects of economic news on public economic behavior may be overrated by corporate decision makers since public economic behavior is more strongly a result of the individual financial situation than the result of the public sentiment on the general economy or the tone of economic news. For media financing, a deteriorated economic situation reflected in a negative economic news tone may at first lead to an increase but may later lead to a decline in advertising income.

References

Adoni, Hanna, and Akiba A. Cohen. 1978. "Television economic news and the social construction of economic reality." *Journal of Communication* 28 (4): 61–70. doi:10.1111/j.1460-2466.1978.tb01657.x.

Adrangi, Bahram, and Joseph Macri. 2011. "Consumer confidence and aggregate consumption expenditures in the United States." *Review of Economics and Finance* (1): 1–18.

Ajzen, Icek. 1985. "From intentions to actions: A theory of planned behavior." In *Action control: From cognition to behavior*, edited by Julius Kuhl and Jürgen Beckmann, 11–39. Berlin, Heidelberg: Springer.

———. 1991. "The theory of planned behavior." *Organizational Behavior and Human Decision Processes* 50 (2): 179–211. doi:10.1016/0749-5978(91)90020-T.

Ajzen, Icek, and Martin Fishbein. 1977. "Attitude-behavior relations: A theoretical analysis and review of empirical research." *Psychological Bulletin* 84 (5): 888–918. doi:10.1037/0033-2909.84.5.888.

———. 1980. *Understanding attitudes and predicting social behavior.* Englewood Cliffs, N.J: Prentice-Hall.

———. 2005. "The influence of attitudes on behavior." In *The handbook of attitudes*, edited by Dolores Albarracín, Blair T. Johnson, and Mark P. Zanna, 173–221. Mahwah, NJ, US: Lawrence Erlbaum Associates Publishers.

Altmeppen, Klaus-Dieter. 2006. *Journalismus und Medien als Organisationen: Leistungen, Strukturen und Management.* Wiesbaden: VS Verlag.

Armitage, Christopher J., and Mark Conner. 2001. "Efficacy of the theory of planned behaviour: A meta-analytic review." *British Journal of Social Psychology* 40 (4): 471–99. doi:10.1348/014466601164939.

Asteriou, Dimitrios, and Stephen G. Hall. 2011. *Applied econometrics.* 2nd ed. Basingstoke: Palgrave Macmillan.

Bachl, Marko. 2009. "Media effects on perceptions of the state of the economy in Germany: Evidence from a Time Series Analysis 1998 – 2007." Paper presented at the annual meeting of the International Communication Association, Chicago, Illinois, USA, May 21.

Bagwell, Kyle. 2001. *The economics of advertising.* The international library of critical writings in economics 136. Cheltenham: Elgar. http://www.gbv.de/dms/hbz/toc/ht013424801.pdf.

Ball-Rokeach, Sandra J., and Melvin L. DeFleur. 1976. "A dependency model of mass-media effects." *Communication Research* 3 (1): 3–21. doi:10.1177/009365027600300101.

Beam, Randal A. 2003. "Content differences between daily newspapers with strong and weak market orientations." *Journalism & Mass Communication Quarterly* 80 (2): 368–90. doi:10.1177/107769900308000209.

Beck, Hanno, and Helmut Wienert. 2009. "Anatomie der Weltwirtschaftskrise: Ursachen und Schuldige." *Aus Politik und Zeitgeschichte* 20: 7–12. http://www.bpb.de/apuz/31998/anatomie-der-weltwirtschaftskrise-ursachen-und-schuldige?p=all. Accessed May 22, 2014.

Behr, Roy L., and Shanto Iyengar. 1985. "Television news, real-world cues, and changes in the public agenda." *Public Opinion Quarterly* 49 (1): 38–57. doi:10.1086/268900.

Blendon, Robert J., John M. Benson, Mollyann Brodie, Richard Morin, Drew E. Altman, Daniel Gitterman, Mario Brossard, and Matt James. 1997. "Bridging the gap between the public's and economists' views of the economy." *The Journal of Economic Perspectives* 11 (3): 105–18. doi:10.2307/2138187.

Blinder, Alan S., and Alan B. Krueger. 2004. "What does the public know about economic policy, and how does it know it?" CEPS Working Paper No. 99. Accessed December 05, 2011. https://www.princeton.edu/ceps/workingpapers/99blinderkrueger.pdf.

Blondheim, Menahem, Elad Segev, and María-Ángeles Cabrera. 2015. "The prominence of weak economies: Factors and trends in global news coverage of economic crisis, 2009–2012." *International Journal of Communication* 9: 46–65.

Blood, Deborah J., and Peter Phillips. 1995. "Recession headline news, consumer sentiment, the state of the economy and presidential popularity: A time series analysis 1989-1993." *International Journal of Public Opinion Research* 7 (1): 2–22. doi:10.1093/ijpor/7.1.2.

Blood, Richard W. 1981. "Unobtrusive issues in the agenda-setting role of the press." Dissertation Paper 64, Mass Communications, Syracuse University.

Bonfadelli, Heinz. 2004. *Medienwirkungsforschung I: Grundlagen und theoretische Perspektiven.* 3rd ed. UTB 2502. Konstanz: UVK.

Brettschneider, Frank. 2003. "Economic affairs, media coverage, and the public's perception of the economy in Germany." In *Communication research and media science in Europe: Perspectives for research and academic training in Europe's changing media reality*, edited by Angela Schorr, 251–70. Berlin: Mouton de Gruyter.

Brosius, Hans-Bernd, and Gabriel Weimann. 1996. "Who sets the agenda: Agenda-setting as a two-step flow." *Communication Research* 23 (5): 561–80. doi:10.1177/009365096023005002.

Carroll, Christopher D. 2003. "Macroeconomic expectations of households and professional forecasters." *Quarterly Journal of Economics* 118 (1): 269–98. doi:10.1162/00335530360535207.

Carroll, Christopher D., Jeffrey C. Fuhrer, and David W. Wilcox. 1994. "Does consumer sentiment forecast household spending? If so, why?" *American Economic Review* 84 (5): 1397–1408. doi:10.2307/2117779.

Chua, Chew L., and Sarantis Tsiaplias. 2009. "Can consumer sentiment and its components forecast Australian GDP and consumption?" *Journal of Forecasting* 28 (8): 698–711. doi:10.1002/for.1120.

Cialdini, Robert B. 2001. *Influence: Science and practice.* 4th ed. Harlow: Pearson Higher Education.

Cochrane, John H. 2015. "Unit roots in English and pictures." Accessed May 20, 2015. http://johnhcochrane.blogspot.ch/2015/04/unit-roots-in-english-and-pictures.html?m=1.

Coleman, James S. 1986. "Social theory, social research, and a theory of action." *American Journal of Sociology* 91 (6): 1309–35. doi:10.2307/2779798.

———. 1990. *Foundations of social theory.* Cambridge, Mass: Belknap Press of Harvard University Press.

Cotsomitis, John A., and Andy C. C. Kwan. 2006. "Can consumer confidence forecast household spending? Evidence from the European commission business and consumer surveys." *Southern Economic Journal* 72 (3): 597–610. doi:10.2307/20111835.

Dailami, Mansoor, and Paul Masson. 2009. "Measures of investor and consumer confidence and policy actions in the current crisis." Accessed January 21, 2014. http://www-wds.worldbank.org/servlet/WDSContentServer/WDSP/IB/2009/07/20/000158349_20090720145703/Rendered/PDF/WPS5007.pdf.

D'Alessio, Dave, and Mike Allen. 2000. "Media bias in presidential elections: A meta-analysis." *Journal of Communication* 50 (4): 133. doi:10.1111/j.1460-2466.2000.tb02866.x.

Davison, W. P. 1983. "The third-person effect in communication." *Public Opinion Quarterly* 47 (1): 1–15. doi:10.1086/268763.

Degenhard, Joachim. 2011. "Konformitätsverhalten und Medien-Kampagnen der Leitmedien in der Politik-Berichterstattung: Eine empirische Studie über Konformitätsverhalten der Leitmedien in der Politik-Berichterstattung zur Klimadebatte 2007/Gesundheitsreformdebatte Juli 2006–März 2007/Arbeitsmarktreformdebatte-Hartz-IV Juli–Dezember 2004." Dissertation. Accessed May 09, 2014. https://eldorado.tu-dortmund.de/bitstream/2003/29143/1/Dissertation.pdf.

Demers, David P., Dennis Craff, Yang-Ho Choi, and Beth M. Pessin. 1989. "Issue obtrusiveness and the agenda-setting effects of national network news." *Communication Research* 16 (6): 793–812. doi:10.1177/009365089016006004.

Desroches, Brigitte, and Marc-André Gosselin. 2004. "Evaluating threshold effects in consumer sentiment." *Southern Economic Journal* 70 (4): 942–52. doi:10.2307/4135281.

Diefenbach, Donald L., and Mark D. West. 2012. "Cultivation and the third-person effect." In *Living with television now: Advances in cultivation theory & research*, edited by Michael Morgan, James Shanahan, and Nancy Signorielli, 329–46. New York: Peter Lang.

Doms, Mark, and Norman Morin. 2004. "Consumer sentiment, the economy, and the news media." FRBSF Working Paper 2004-09. Accessed June 16, 2014. http://fedinprint.org/items/fedfwp/2004-09.html.

Döpke, Jörg, Jonas Dovern, Ulrich Fritsche, and Jiri Slacalek. 2008. "Sticky information Phillips curves:." *Journal of Money, Credit & Banking* 40 (7): 1513–20. doi:10.1111/j.1538-4616.2008.00169.x.

Doyle, Gillian. 2006. "Financial news journalism: A post-Enron analysis of approaches towards economic and financial news production in the UK." *Journalism* 7 (4): 433–52. doi:10.1177/1464884906068361.

Dräger, Lena. 2011. "Inflation perceptions and expectations in Sweden - Are media reports the 'missing link'?" Accessed February 17, 2012. http://www.kof.ethz.ch/de/publikationen/p/kof-working-papers/273/.

Easaw, Joshy, and Atanu Ghoshray. 2010. "News and households: subjective macroeconomic expectations." *Journal of Macroeconomics* 32 (1): 469–75. doi:10.1016/j.jmacro.2009.12.002.

Easaw, Joshy Z., Dean Garratt, and Saeed M. Heravi. 2005. "Does consumer sentiment accurately forecast UK household consumption? Are there any comparisons to be made with the US?" *Journal of Macroeconomics* 27 (3): 517–32. doi:10.1016/j.jmacro.2004.03.001.

Easaw, Joshy Z., and Saeed M. Heravi. 2004. "Evaluating consumer sentiments as predictors of UK household consumption behavior." *International Journal of Forecasting* 20 (4): 671–81. doi:10.1016/j.ijforecast.2003.12.006.

Ecke, Oliver. 2011. "Relevanz der Medien für die Meinungsbildung: Empirische Grundlagen zur Ermittlung der Wertigkeit der Mediengattungen bei der Meinungsbildung." Accessed November 26, 2013. https://www.blm.de/apps/documentbase/data/pdf1/Medienkonzentration.pdf.

Eilders, Christiane. 2002. "Conflict and consonance in media opinion: Political positions of five German quality newspapers." *European Journal of Communication* 17 (1): 25–63. doi:10.1177/0267323102017001606.

Enders, Walter. 2010. *Applied econometric time series.* 3rd ed. Wiley series in probability and statistics. Hoboken, NJ: Wiley.

Eppright, David R., Nestor M. Arguea, and William L. Huth. 1998. "Aggregate consumer expectation indexes as indicators of future consumer expenditures." *Journal of Economic Psychology* 19 (2): 215–35. doi:10.1016/S0167-4870(98)00005-1.

Erbring, Lutz, Eldie N. Goldenberg, and Arthur H. Miller. 1980. "Front-page news and real-world cues: A new look at agenda-setting by the media." *American Journal of Political Science* 24 (1): 16.

Esser, Hartmut. 1993. *Soziologie: Allgemeine Grundlagen.* Frankfurt/Main, New York: Campus.

———. 1999. *Soziologie. Spezielle Grundlagen.* Frankfurt a.M., New York: Campus Verlag. Band 1: Situationslogik und Handeln.

European Commission. 2014. "The joint harmonised EU programme of business and consumer surveys: User guide." Accessed January 08, 2015. http://ec.europa.eu/economy_finance/db_indicators/surveys/documents/bcs_user_guide_en.pdf.

Fair, Ray C. 2004. *Estimating how the macroeconomy works.* Cambridge, Mass: Harvard University Press. Accessed January 21, 2014. http://fairmodel.econ.yale.edu/rayfair/pdf/2003A.HTM.

Farmer, Roger E. A. 1999. *The macroeconomics of self-fulfilling prophecies.* 2nd ed. Cambridge, Mass: MIT Press.

Fazio, Russel. 1986. "How do attitudes guide behavior?" In *Handbook of motivation and cognition,* edited by Richard M. Sorrentino, 204–43. New York: Guilford Press.

Fields, James M., and Howard Schuman. 1976. "Public beliefs about the beliefs of the public." *Public Opinion Quarterly* 40 (4): 427. doi:10.1086/268330.

Fuchs, Victor R., Alan B. Krueger, and James M. Poterba. 1998. "Economists' views about parameters, values, and policies: Survey results in labor and public economics." *Journal of Economic Literature* 36 (3): 1387–1425. doi:10.2307/2564804.

Fuhrer, Jeffrey C. 1993. "What role does consumer sentiment play in the U.S. macroeconomy?" *New England Economic Review,* 32–44.

Fuller, Dan, and Doris Geide-Stevenson. 2003. "Consensus among economists: Revisited." *Journal of Economic Education* 34 (4): 369–87. doi:10.2307/30042564.

Funkhouser, G. Ray. 1973. "The issues of the Sixties: An exploratory study in the dynamics of public opinion." *Public Opinion Quarterly* 37 (1): 62. doi:10.1086/268060.

Galbraith, John K. 1967. *The new industrial state.* 3rd ed. Boston: Houghton Mifflin.

Gelper, Sarah, Aurélie Lemmens, and Christophe Croux. 2007. "Consumer sentiment and consumer spending: decomposing the Granger causal relationship in the time domain." *Applied Economics* 39 (1): 1–11. doi:10.1080/00036840500427791.

Gerbner, George. 1969. "Toward "Cultural Indicators": The Analysis of Mass Mediated Public Message Systems." *AV Communication Review* 17 (2): 137–48. doi:10.2307/30217499.

Ghanem, Salma I. 1997. "Filling in the tapestry: The second level of agenda setting." In *Communication and democracy,* edited by Maxwell E. McCombs, Donald L. Shaw, and David H. Weaver, 3–14. Mahwah, N.J, London: Lawrence Erlbaum.

Goidel, Kirby, Stephen Procopio, Dek Terrell, and H. D. Wu. 2010. "Sources of economic news and economic expectations." *American Politics Research* 38 (4): 759–77. doi:10.1177/1532673X09355671.

Goidel, Robert K., and Ronald E. Langley. 1995. "Media coverage of the economy and aggregate economic evaluations: Uncovering evidence of indirect media effects." *Political Research Quarterly* 48 (2): 313–28. doi:10.1177/106591299504800205.

Golan, Guy, and Wayne Wanta. 2001. "Second-level agenda setting in the new hampshire primary: A comparison of coverage in three newspapers and public perceptions of candidates." *Journalism & Mass Communication Quarterly* 78 (2): 247–59. doi:10.1177/107769900107800203.

Granger, C.W.J., and P. Newbold. 1974. "Spurious regressions in econometrics." *Journal of Econometrics* 2 (2): 111–20. doi:10.1016/0304-4076(74)90034-7.

Granger, Clive W. 1969. "Investigating causal relations by econometric models and cross-spectral methods." *Econometrica* 37 (3): 424–38. doi:10.2307/1912791.

Greenberg, Bradley S. 1964. "Person-to-person communication in the diffusion of news events." *Journalism Quarterly* 41:489–94.
Greve, Jens, Annette Schnabel, and Rainer Schützeichel. 2009. "Das Makro-Mikro-Makro-Modell der soziologischen Erklärung – zur Einleitung." In *Das Mikro-Makro-Modell der soziologischen Erklärung*, edited by Jens Greve, Annette Schnabel, and Rainer Schützeichel, 7–17: VS Verlag.
Grossarth-Maticek, Jan, and Johannes Mayr. 2008. "Medienberichte als Konjunkturindikator." *ifo Schnelldienst* 61 (7): 17–29. http://www.cesifo-group.de/DocDL/ifosd_2008_7_3.pdf. Accessed February 19, 2015.
Gunther, Albert C. 1998. "The persuasive press inference: Effects of mass media on perceived public opinion." *Communication Research* 25 (5): 486–504. doi:10.1177/009365098025005002.
Gunther, Albert C., and J. D. Storey. 2003. "The influence of presumed influence." *Journal of Communication* 53 (2): 199–215. doi:10.1111/j.1460-2466.2003.tb02586.x.
Gustafsson, Karl E. 2006. "Advertising and the development of media: The forgotten connection." *Journal of Media Business Studies* 3 (1): 19–32. doi:10.1080/16522354.2006.11073437.
Hackett, Robert A. 1984. "Decline of a paradigm? Bias and objectivity in news media studies." *Critical Studies in Mass Communication* 1 (3): 329. doi:10.1080/15295038409360036.
Hagen, Lutz. 2004. "Agenda-setting unemployment: Media-effects upon perceptions of sociotropic versus egotropic aspects of issue-salience." Paper presented at the annual meeting of the International Communication Association, New Orleans, LA, USA, May 27.
Hagen, Lutz M. 2005. *Konjunkturnachrichten, Konjunkturklima und Konjunktur: Wie sich die Wirtschaftsberichterstattung der Massenmedien, Stimmungen der Bevölkerung und die aktuelle Wirtschaftslage wechselseitig beeinflussen. Eine transaktionale Analyse.* Köln: von Halem.
Haller, H. B., and Helmut Norpoth. 1997. "Reality bites: News exposure and economic opinion." *Public Opinion Quarterly* 61 (4): 555–75. doi:10.1086/297817.
Halloran, James D., Philip R. C. Elliott, Graham Murdock, and Grant Noble. 1970. *Demonstrations and communication: A case study.* Penguin special. Harmondsworth: Penguin Books.
Hamilton, James T. 2004. *All the news that's fit to sell: How the market transforms information into news.* Princeton, NJ: Princeton University Press.
Hanitzsch, Thomas, Maria Anikina, Rosa Berganza, Incilay Cangoz, Mihai Coman, Basyouni Hamada, Folker Hanusch et al. 2010. "Modeling perceived influences on journalism: Evidence from a cross-national survey of journalists." *Journalism & Mass Communication Quarterly* 87 (1): 5–22. doi:10.1177/107769901008700101.
Hanitzsch, Thomas, and Claudia Mellado. 2011. "What shapes the news around the world? How journalists in eighteen countries perceive influences on their work." *International Journal of Press/Politics* 16 (3): 404–26. doi:10.1177/1940161211407334.
Harrington, David E. 1989. "Economic news on television: The determinants of coverage." *Public Opinion Quarterly* 53 (1): 17. doi:10.1086/269139.
Harrison, Sharon G., and Mark Weder. 2006. "Did sunspot forces cause the Great Depression?" *Journal of Monetary Economics* 53 (7): 1327–39. doi:10.1016/j.jmoneco.2005.07.018.
Heim, John J. 2009. "Does consumer confidence, as measured by the Conference Board's Index Of Consumer Confidence, affect demand for consumer and investment goods (or just proxy for things that do)?" Accessed January 21, 2014. http://www.economics.rpi.edu/workingpapers/rpi0904.pdf.
Hester, Joe B., and Rhonda Gibson. 2003. "The economy and second level agenda setting: A time-series analysis of economic news and public opinion about the economy." *Journalism & Mass Communication Quarterly* 80 (1): 73–90.

Hetsroni, Amir, and Hila Lowenstein. 2012. "Cultivation and agenda-setting." In *Living with television now: Advances in cultivation theory & research*, edited by Michael Morgan, James Shanahan, and Nancy Signorielli, 307–28. New York: Peter Lang.

Hollanders, David, and Rens Vliegenthart. 2011. "The influence of negative newspaper coverage on consumer confidence: The Dutch case." *Journal of Economic Psychology* 32 (3): 367–73. doi:10.1016/j.joep.2011.01.003.

Hsu, Maxwell K., Ali F. Darrat, Zhong Maosen, and Salah S. Abosedra. 2002. "Does advertising stimulate sales or mainly deliver signals? A multivariate analysis." *International Journal of Advertising* 21 (2): 175–95. doi:10.1080/02650487.2002.11104925.

ifo. 2014a. "Ifo World Economic Survey." Accessed April 23, 2015. http://www.cesifo-group.de/ifoHome/facts/Survey-Results/World-Economic-Survey.html.

———. 2014b. "Ifo World Economic Survey: Become a member of the Ifo WES expert group!". Accessed April 23, 2015. http://www.cesifo-group.de/ifoHome/facts/Survey-Results/World-Economic-Survey/WES-Expert-Group.html.

Ivanova, Detelina, and Kajal Lahiri. 2001. "When should we care about consumer sentiment? Evidence from linear and Markov-switching models." *Indian Economic Review* 36 (1): 153–69. doi:10.2307/29794230.

IVW. 2013. "Tageszeitungen Gesamtliste." Accessed January 10, 2013. www.ivw.eu.

Iyengar, Shanto, and Donald R. Kinder. 1987. *News that matters: Television and American opinion*. American politics and political economy series. Chicago: University of Chicago Press.

Jäckel, Michael. 2007. "„...dass man nichts zu wählen hat": Die Kontroverse um den Homo Oeconomicus." In *Journalismustheorie: Next Generation: Soziologische Grundlegung und theoretische Innovation*, edited by Klaus-Dieter Altmeppen, Thomas Hanitzsch, and Carsten Schlüter, 71–95. Wiesbaden: VS Verlag.

Jarren, Otfried, and Martina Vogel. 2009. "Gesellschaftliche Selbstbeobachtung und Ko-Orientierung: Die Leitmedien der modernen Gesellschaft." In *Leitmedien: Konzepte - Relevanz - Geschichte*, edited by Daniel Müller, 71–92. Medienumbrüche 31-32. Bielefeld: Transcript.

Jensen, Jakob D., and Ryan J. Hurley. 2005. "Third-person effects and the environment: Social distance, social desirability, and presumed behavior." *Journal of Communication* 55 (2): 242–56. doi:10.1111/j.1460-2466.2005.tb02670.x.

Jepperson, Ronald L. 2002. "The development and application of sociological neoinstitutionalism." In *New directions in contemporary sociological theory*, edited by Joseph Berger and Morris Zelditch, 229–66. Lanham, MD: Rowman & Littlefield Publishers.

Johnson, Bair T., Gregory R. Maio, and Aaron Smith-McLallen. 2005. "Communication and attitude change: Causes, processes, and effects." In *The handbook of attitudes*, edited by Dolores Albarracín, Blair T. Johnson, and Mark P. Zanna, 617–69. Mahwah, NJ, US: Lawrence Erlbaum Associates Publishers.

Jones, John P. 2007. *When ads work: New proof that advertising triggers sales*. 2nd ed. Armonk, N.Y: Sharpe.

Ju, Youngkee. 2008. "The asymmetry in economic news coverage and its impact on public perception in South Korea." *International Journal of Public Opinion Research* 20 (2): 237–49. doi:10.1093/ijpor/edn021.

Kahneman, Daniel. 2003. "Maps of bounded rationality: Psychology for behavioral economics." *American Economic Review* 93 (5): 1449–75. doi:10.1257/000282803322655392.

Kahneman, Daniel, and Dan Lovallo. 1993. "Timid choices and bold forecasts: A cognitive perspective on risk taking." *Management Science* 39 (1): 17–31. doi:10.1287/mnsc.39.1.17.

Kalogeropoulos, Antonis, Erik Albæk, Claes H. de Vreese, and Arjen van Dalen. 2015. "The predictors of economic sophistication: Media, interpersonal communication and negative economic experiences." *European Journal of Communication*. doi:10.1177/0267323115582149.

Kater, Ulrich. 2008. *Die 100 wichtigsten Konjunkturindikatoren weltweit*. 2nd ed. Wiesbaden: Cometis.

Katona, George. 1951. *Psychological analysis of economic behavior*. New York: McGraw-Hill.

———. 1957. "Public Opinion and Economic Research." *Public Opinion Quarterly* 21 (1): 117–28. doi:10.1086/266691.

———. 1968. "Consumer behavior: Theory and findings on expectations and aspirations." *The American Economic Review* 58 (2): 19–30. doi:10.2307/1831793.

———. 1974. "Psychology and consumer economics." *Journal of Consumer Research* 1 (1): 1–8. doi:10.2307/2488948.

———. 1975. *Psychological economics*. New York: Elsevier Scientific Pub. Co.

Katz, Elihu. 1957. "The two-step flow of communication: An up-to-date report on an hypothesis." *The Public Opinion Quarterly* 21 (1): 61–78. doi:10.2307/2746790.

Kepplinger, Hans M. 2007. "Reciprocal effects: Toward a theory of mass media effects on decision makers." *Harvard International Journal of Press/Politics* 12 (2): 3–23. doi:10.1177/1081180x07299798.

———. 2010. *Medieneffekte*. Theorie und Praxis öffentlicher Kommunikation 4. Wiesbaden: VS Verlag.

———. 2011. "Der Ereignisbegriff in der Publizistikwissenschaft." In *Realitätskonstruktionen*, edited by Hans M. Kepplinger, 67–83. Wiesbaden: VS Verlag.

Kienzler, Stephanie, and Juliane Lischka. 2013. "Von proaktiv zu reaktiv? Implikationen einer Makro-Analyse zum Werbeverhalten in Deutschland 1991-2009." In *Wert und Werte der Marketingkommunikation*, edited by Thomas Schierl and Jörg Tropp, 153–71. Köln: von Halem.

———. 2015. "Planung von Werbeausgaben." In *Handbuch Werbeforschung*, edited by Gabriele Siegert, Werner Wirth, Patrick Weber, and Juliane A. Lischka, 149–72. Wiesbaden: VS Verlag.

Kienzler, Stephanie, Juliane Lischka, and Gabriele Siegert. 2012. "Einflussfaktoren auf unternehmerische Werbeentscheidungen - eine länderübergreifende Studie." In *Qualitäten der Werbung - Qualitäten der Werbeforschung*, edited by Hannes Haas and Katharina Lobinger, 172–94. Köln: von Halem.

Kittel, Bernhard, and Hannes Winner. 2005. "How reliable is pooled analysis in political economy? The globalization-welfare state nexus revisited." *European Journal of Political Research* 44 (2): 269–93. doi:10.1111/j.1475-6765.2005.00228.x.

Klein, Malcom W., and Nathan Maccoby. 1954. "Newspaper objectivity in the 1952 campaign." *Journalism Quarterly* 31: 285–96.

Kleinnijenhuis, Jan, Friederike Schultz, and Dirk Oegema. 2015. "Frame complexity and the financial crisis: A comparison of the United States, the United Kingdom, and Germany in the period 2007-2012." *Journal of Communication* 65 (1): 1–23. doi:10.1111/jcom.12141.

Koch, Thomas, and Thomas Zerback. 2013. "Helpful or harmful? How frequent repetition affects perceived statement credibility." *Journal of Communication* 63 (6): 993–1010. doi:10.1111/jcom.12063.

Krause, Birgit, and Benjamin Fretwurst. 2007. "Kurzfristige Agenda-Setting-Effekte von Fernsehnachrichten: Eine Zeitreihenanalyse am Beispiel Ausländerfeindlichkeit und Rechtsradikalismus." In *Fortschritte der politischen Kommunikationsforschung: Festschrift für Lutz Erbring*, edited by Birgit Krause, Benjamin Fretwurst, and Jens Vogelgesang, 171–96. Forschung Kommunikation. Wiesbaden: VS Verlag.

Krause, Birgit, and Volker Gehrau. 2007. "Das Paradox der Medienwirkung auf Nichtnutzer." *Publizistik* 52 (2): 191–209. doi:10.1007/s11616-007-0083-1.

Lamla, Michael J., and Sarah M. Lein. 2008. "The role of media for consumers' inflation expectation formation: KOF Working Paper Nr. 201." Accessed December 22, 2011. http://kof.ethz.ch/de/publikationen/p/kof-working-papers/201/.

Lazarsfeld, Paul F., Bernard Berelson, and Hazel Gaudet. 1944. *The people's choice: How the voter makes up his mind in a presidental campaign.* New York, Berlin: Spiess.

Lee, GangHoeng. 2004. "Reconciling 'cognitive priming' vs 'obtrusive contingency' hypotheses: An analytical model of media agenda-setting effects." *International Communication Gazette* 66 (2): 151–66. doi:10.1177/0016549204041475.

Levanon, Gad. 2010. "Evaluating and comparing leading and coincident economic indicators." *Business Economics* 45 (1): 16–27. doi:10.1057/be.2009.29.

Lippmann, Walter. 1922. *Public opinion.* New York: Harcourt, Brace and Company.

Lischka, Juliane A. 2014a. "Different revenue incentives, different content? Comparing economic news before and during the financial crisis in German public and commercial news outlets over time." *European Journal of Communication* 29 (5): 549–66. doi:10.1177/0267323114538851.

———. 2014b. *Sentiments on the economy: How economic news affects collective economic expectations and behavior.* Cumulative dissertation thesis. Zurich: University of Zurich. Accessed April 15, 2015. http://opac.nebis.ch/F/?local_base=NEBIS&CON_LNG=GER&func=find-b&find_code=SYS&request=010348503.

———. 2015. "What follows what? Relations between economic indicators, economic expectations of the public, and news on the general economy and unemployment in Germany, 2002–2011." *Journalism & Mass Communication Quarterly* 92 (2): 374–98. doi:10.1177/1077699015574098.

Lischka, Juliane A., Stephanie Kienzler, and Ulrike Mellmann. 2014. "Sales drive advertising expenditures: Evidence for consumer packaged and durable goods in Germany." *International Journal of Marketing Studies* 6 (1): 31–44. doi:10.5539/ijms.v6n1p31.

Lischka, Juliane A., and Wolfgang Seufert. 2015. "Messung von Werbewirkungen auf Makroebene." In *Handbuch Werbeforschung,* edited by Gabriele Siegert, Werner Wirth, Patrick Weber, and Juliane A. Lischka, 517–46. Wiesbaden: VS Verlag.

Lischka, Juliane A., and Gabriele Siegert. 2013. "Beeinflussen Wirtschaftsnachrichten auch Wirtschaftserwartungen von Experten? Die Prognosequalität von öffentlich-rechtlichen und Service public Wirtschaftsnachrichten für Erwartungen von Wirtschaftsexperten in Deutschland und in der Schweiz." *Studies in Communication Sciences* 13 (2): 174–84. doi:10.1016/j.scoms.2013.09.002.

Lowry, Dennis T. 2008. "Network TV news framing of good vs. bad economic news under democrat and republican presidents: A lexical analysis of political bias." *Journalism & Mass Communication Quarterly* 85 (3): 483–98. doi:10.1177/107769900808500301.

Ludvigson, Sydney C. 2004. "Consumer confidence and consumer spending." *The Journal of Economic Perspectives* 18 (2): 29–50. doi:10.1257/0895330041371222.

Lutkepohl, Helmut. 2004. "Vector autoregressive and vector error correction models." In *Applied time series econometrics,* edited by Helmut Lutkepohl and Markus Kratzig, 86–158: Themes in Modern Econometrics; Cambridge; New York and Melbourne; Cambridge University Press.

Maher, Micheal T. 2001. "Framing: An emerging paradigm or a phase of agenda setting?" In *Framing public life: Perspectives on media and our understanding of the social world,* edited by Stephen D. Reese, Oscar H. Gandy, and August E. Grant, 83–94. Mahwah, NJ: Lawrence Erlbaum.

Manning, Paul. 2013. "Financial journalism, news sources and the banking crisis." *Journalism* 14 (2): 173–89. doi:10.1177/1464884912448915.

Marron, Maria B., Zeny Sarabia-Panol, Marianne D. Sison, Sandhya Rao, and Ray Niekamp. 2010. "The scorecard on reporting of the global financial crisis." *Journalism Studies* 11 (2): 270–83. doi:10.1080/14616700903538413.
Mast, Claudia. 2012. *Neuorientierung im Wirtschaftjournalismus: Redaktionelle Strategien und Publikumserwartungen.* Wiesbaden: Springer VS.
Matthes, Jörg. 2006. "The need for orientation towards news media: Revising and validating a classic concept." *International Journal of Public Opinion Research* 18 (4): 422–44. doi:10.1093/ijpo/edh118.
———. 2008. "Need for orientation as a predictor of agenda-setting effects: Causal evidence from a two-wave panel study." *International Journal of Public Opinion Research* 20 (4): 440–53. doi:10.1093/ijpor/edn042.
Maurer, Markus. 2004. "Das Paradox der Medienwirkungsforschung: Verändern Massenmedien die Bevölkerungsmeinung, ohne Einzelne zu beeinflussen?" *Publizistik* 49 (4): 405–22. doi:10.1007/s11616-004-0108-y.
McCombs, Maxwell E. 1992. "Explorers and surveyors: Expanding strategies for agenda-setting research." *Journalism Quarterly* 69 (4): 813–24. doi:10.1177/107769909206900402.
McCombs, Maxwell E., and Salma I. Ghanem. 2001. "The convergence of agenda setting and framing." In *Framing public life: Perspectives on media and our understanding of the social world*, edited by Stephen D. Reese, Oscar H. Gandy, and August E. Grant, 67–81. Mahwah, NJ: Lawrence Erlbaum.
McCombs, Maxwell E., and Donald L. Shaw. 1972. "The agenda-setting function of mass media." *Public Opinion Quarterly* 36 (2): 176–87. doi:10.1086/267990.
———. 1993. "The evolution of agenda-setting research: Twenty-five years in the marketplace of ideas." *Journal of Communication* 43 (2): 58. doi:10.1111/j.1460-2466.1993.tb01262.x.
McQuail, Denis. 1992. *Media performance: Mass communication and the public interest.* London: Sage.
Mishkin, Frederic S. 1978. "Consumer sentiment and spending on durable goods." *Brookings Papers on Economic Activity* (1): 217–31.
Mutz, Diana C. 1992. "Mass media and the depoliticization of personal experience." *American Journal of Political Science* 36 (2): 483–508. doi:10.2307/2111487.
———. 1994. "Contextualizing personal experience: The role of the mass media." *Journal of Politics* 56 (3): 689. doi:10.2307/2132188.
Nelissen, Paul, Ruben Konig, and Karsten Renckstorf. 2008. "Occupational position and consumption of news: A research note." *Communications* 33 (4). doi:10.1515/COMM.2008.029.
Neuman, W. R., Lauren Guggenheim, S. Mo Jang, and Soo Y. Bae. 2014. "The dynamics of public attention: Agenda-setting theory meets big data." *Journal of Communication* 64 (2): 193–214. doi:10.1111/jcom.12088.
Nguyen Vu, Hong N. 2010. "Money matters: A cross-national study of economic influences on TV news." Dissertation, Universität Zürich.
Nguyen Vu, Hong N., and Volker Gehrau. 2010. "Agenda diffusion: An integrated model of agenda setting and interpersonal communication." *Journalism & Mass Communication Quarterly* 87 (1): 100–116. doi:10.1177/107769901008700106.
Noelle-Neumann, Elisabeth. 1973. "Kumulation, Konsonanz und Öffentlichkeitseffekt. Ein neuer Ansatz zur Analyse der Wirkung der Massenmedien." *Publizistik* 18: 26–55.
———. 1987. "The public as a prophet: Findings from continuous survey research and their importance for early diagnostics of economic growth." In *The 40th ESOMAR Marketing Research Congress, Montreux, 13th-17th September 1987*, edited by ESOMAR, 279–96. Amsterdam: ESOMAR, European Society for Opinion and Marketing Research.

Noelle-Neumann, Elisabeth, and Rainer Mathes. 1987. "The 'event as event' and the 'event as news': The significance of 'consonance' for media effects research." *European Journal of Communication* 2 (4): 391–414. doi:10.1177/0267323187002004002.
Oh, Seonghwan, and Michael Waldman. 1990. "The macroeconomic effects of false announcements." *Quarterly Journal of Economics* 105 (4): 1017–34. doi:10.2307/2937883.
Östgaard, Einar. 1965. "Factors influencing the flow of news." *Journal of Peace Research* 2 (1): 39–63. doi:10.1177/002234336500200103.
Perloff, Richard M. 1989. "Ego-involvement and the third person effect of televised news coverage." *Communication Research* 16 (2): 236. doi:10.1177/009365089016002004.
———. 1993. "Third-person effect research 1983–1992: A review and synthesis." *International Journal of Public Opinion Research* 5 (2): 167–84. doi:10.1093/ijpor/5.2.167.
Peter, Jochen. 2003. "Konsonanz 30 Jahre später." *Publizistik* 48 (2): 190–208. doi:10.1007/s11616-003-0042-4.
———. 2004. "Our long 'return to the concept of powerful mass media'-- A cross-national comparative investigation of the effects of consonant media coverage." *International Journal of Public Opinion Research* 16 (2): 144–68. doi:10.1093/ijpor/16.2.144.
Picard, Robert G. 2001. "Effects of recessions on advertising expenditures: An exploratory study of economic downturns in nine developed nations." *Journal of Media Economics* 14 (1): 1–14. doi:10.1207/S15327736ME1401_01.
———. 2004. "Commercialism and newspaper quality." *Newspaper Research Journal* 25 (1): 54–65.
Picard, Robert G., Meera Selva, and Diego Bironzo. 2014. "Media coverage of banking and financial news." Accessed March 03, 2015. https://reutersinstitute.politics.ox.ac.uk/fileadmin/documents/Publications/Other_publications/Media_Coverage_of_Banking_and_Financial_News.pdf.
Potter, W. J. 2014. "A critical analysis of cultivation theory." *Journal of Communication* 64 (6): 1015–36. doi:10.1111/jcom.12128.
Praet, Peter, and Jozef Vuchelen. 1984. "The contribution of E.C. consumer surveys in forecasting consumer expenditures: An econometric analysis for four major countries." *Journal of Economic Psychology* 5 (2): 101–24. doi:10.1016/0167-4870(84)90001-1.
Prat, Andrea, and David Strömberg. 2012. "The political economy of mass media." In *Advances in economics and econometrics*, edited by Daron Acemoglu, Manuel Arellano, and Eddie Dekel, 135–87. Econometric Society monographs 49. Cambridge: Cambridge University Press.
Quiring, Oliver. 2004. *Wirtschaftsberichterstattung und Wahlen*. Konstanz: UVK.
Quiring, Oliver, and Mathias Weber. 2012. "Between usefulness and legitimacy: Media coverage of governmental intervention during the financial crisis and selected effects." *International Journal of Press/Politics* 17 (3): 294–315. doi:10.1177/1940161212442957.
Rapoport, Ronald B. 1982. "Sex differences in attitude expression: A generational explanation." *Public Opinion Quarterly* 46 (1): 86. doi:10.1086/268701.
Räth, Norbert. 2009. "Rezessionen in historischer Betrachtung." *Wirtschaft und Statistik* (3): 203–8. https://www.destatis.de/DE/Publikationen/WirtschaftStatistik/Monatsausgaben/WistaMaerz09.pdf?__blob=publicationFile. Accessed March 22, 2014.
Reinemann, Carsten. 2007. "Subjektiv rationale Akteure: Das Potenzial handlungstheoretischer Erklärungen für die Journalismusforschung." In *Journalismustheorie: Next Generation: Soziologische Grundlegung und theoretische Innovation*, edited by Klaus-Dieter Altmeppen, Thomas Hanitzsch, and Carsten Schlüter, 47–67. Wiesbaden: VS Verlag.
Robertson, John W. 2010. "The last days of free market hegemony? UK TV news coverage of economic issues in spring 2008." *Media, Culture & Society* 32 (3): 517–29. doi:10.1177/0163443710361659.

Rössler, Patrick. 1997. *Agenda-Setting: Theoretische Annahmen und empirische Evidenzen einer Medienwirkungshypothese.* Studien zur Kommunikationswissenschaft 27. Opladen: Westdeutscher Verlag.
Russi, Loris. 2013. *Ökonomische Bedingungen publizistischer Vielfalt: Eine theoretische Modellierung und Fuzzy Set Analyse der Beziehung von Wettbewerb und Produktdifferenzierung in europäischen Zeitungsmärkten.* Baden-Baden: Nomos.
Saltiel, John, and Joseph Woelfel. 1975. "Inertia in cognitive processes: The role of accumulated information in attitude change." *Human Communication Research* 1 (4): 333–44. doi:10.1111/j.1468-2958.1975.tb00282.x.
Salyer, Kevin D., and Steven M. Sheffrin. 1998. "Spotting sunspots: Some evidence in support of models with self-fulfilling prophecies." *Journal of Monetary Economics* 42 (3): 511–23. doi:10.1016/S0304-3932(98)00037-3.
Schenk, Michael. 1997. "Massenkommunikation und ihre Wirkungen." In *Massenkommunikation: Ergebnisse und Perspektiven,* edited by Hermann Fünfgeld, Claudia Mast, and Gerhard Maletzke, 155–68. Opladen: Westdeutscher Verlag.
Scherer, Helmut. 1990. *Massenmedien, Meinungsklima und Einstellung: Eine Untersuchung zur Theorie der Schweigespirale.* Studien zur Sozialwissenschaft. Wiesbaden: VS Verlag.
Scheufele, Bertram. 1999. *Zeitreihenanalysen in der Kommunikationsforschung: Eine praxisorientierte Einführung in die uni- und multivariate Zeitreihenanalyse mit SPSS for Windows.* Stuttgart: Edition 451.
———. 2003. *Frames - Framing - Framing-Effekte: Theoretische und methodische Grundlegung des Framing-Ansatzes sowie empirische Befunde zur Nachrichtenproduktion.* Wiesbaden: Westdeutscher Verlag.
———. 2008. "Das Erklärungsdilemma der Medienwirkungsforschung: Eine Logik zur theoretischen und methodischen Modellierung von Medienwirkungen auf die Meso- und Makro-Ebene." *Publizistik* 53 (3): 339–61. doi:10.1007/PL00022227.
Schifferes, Steve. 2011. "The financial crisis and the UK media." In *Bad news: How America's business press missed the story of the century,* edited by Anya Schiffrin, 148–78. New York: New Press.
Schifferes, Steve, and Stephen Coulter. 2013. "Downloading disaster: BBC news online coverage of the global financial crisis." *Journalism* 14 (2): 228–52. doi:10.1177/1464884912460171.
Schiffrin, Anya, ed. 2011a. *Bad news: How America's business press missed the story of the century.* New York: New Press.
———. 2011b. "The U.S. press and the financial crisis." In *Bad news: How America's business press missed the story of the century,* edited by Anya Schiffrin, 1–21. New York: New Press.
Schirwitz, Beate. 2009. "A comprehensive German business cycle chronology." *Empir Econ* 37 (2): 287–301. doi:10.1007/s00181-008-0233-y.
Schulz, Winfried. 1976. *Die Konstruktion von Realität in den Nachrichtenmedien: Analyse der aktuellen Berichterstattung.* Freiburg (Breisgau) & München: Alber.
Sei-Hill, Kim, Dietram A. Scheufele, and James Shanahan. 2002. "Think about it this way: Attribute agenda-setting function of the press and the public's evaluation of a local issue." *Journalism & Mass Communication Quarterly* 79 (1): 7–25. doi:10.1177/1748048511426991.
Shaw, Donald L., and Maxwell McCombs. 1977. *The emergence of American political issues: The agenda-setting function of the press.* St.Paul: West Publishing Co.
Shehata, Adam, and Jesper Strömbäck. 2011. "A matter of context: A comparative study of media environments and news consumption gaps in Europe." *Political Communication* 28 (1): 110–34. doi:10.1080/10584609.2010.543006.

———. 2013. "Not (Yet) a new era of minimal effects: A study of agenda setting at the aggregate and individual levels." *International Journal of Press/Politics* 18 (2): 234–55. doi:10.1177/1940161212473831.
Sheppard, Blair H., Jon Hartwick, and Paul R. Warshaw. 1988. "The theory of reasoned action: A meta-analysis of past research with recommendations for modifications and future research." *Journal of Consumer Research* 15 (3): 325–43. doi:10.2307/2489467.
Shiller, Robert J. 2005. *Irrational exuberance.* 2nd ed. Princeton: Princeton University Press.
Shoemaker, Pamela J., and Stephen D. Reese. 1996. *Mediating the message: Theories of influences on mass media content.* 2nd ed. White Plains, NY: Longman.
Siegert, Gabriele, Ulrike Mellmann, Stephanie Kienzler, and Juliane Lischka. 2012. "Wirtschaftskrise - Werbewirtschaftskrise - Medienkrise? Konjunkturell und strukturell bedingte Veränderungen der Werbung und ihre Folgen für die Medien." In *Gehen in den Leuchttürmen die Lichter aus? Was aus den Schweizer Leitmedien wird,* edited by Werner A. Meier, Heinz Bonfadelli, and Josef Trappel, 161–88. Münster: Lit.
Simon, Herbert A. 1956. "Rational choice and the structure of the environment." *Psychological Review* 63 (2): 129–38. doi:10.1037/h0042769.
———. 1987. "Making management decisions: The role of intuition and emotion." *Academy of Management Executive* 1 (1): 57–64. doi:10.5465/AME.1987.4275905.
Sims, Christopher. 1980. "Macroeconomics and reality." *Econometrica* 48 (1): 1–48. doi:10.2307/1912017.
Singletary, Michael W., Raymond Boland, William Izzard, and Terry Rosser. 1983. "How accurate are news magazines' forecasts?" *Journalism & Mass Communication Quarterly* 60 (2): 342–44. doi:10.1177/107769908306000222.
Soley, Lawrence C., and Robert L. Craig. 1992. "Advertising pressures on newspapers: A survey." *Journal of Advertising* 21 (4): 1–10. doi:10.1080/00913367.1992.10673381.
Sommer, Katharina. 2013. "Wirkung von Wirtschaftsberichterstattung – Eine Systematisierung." In *Handbuch Medienwirkungsforschung,* edited by Wolfgang Schweiger and Andreas Fahr, 369–84. Wiesbaden: Springer Fachmedien.
Sommer, Katharina, Sabine Einwiller, Diana Ingenhoff, and Norbert Winistörfer. 2010. "Wirtschaftsberichterstattung im Rundfunk der Schweiz: Eine inhaltsanalytische Untersuchung zu Unterschieden zwischen den Sprachregionen." *Studies in Communication Sciences* 10 (2): 27–50.
Soroka, Stuart N. 2006. "Good news and bad news: Asymmetric responses to economic information." *Journal of Politics* 68 (2): 372–85. doi:10.1111/j.1468-2508.2006.00413.x.
Spachmann, Klaus. 2005. *Wirtschaftsjournalismus in der Presse: Theorie und Empirie.* Medien und Märkte 14. Konstanz: UVK. Zugl. Hohenheim, Univ., Diss., 2004.
Starr, Martha A. 2012. "Consumption, sentiment, and economic news." *Economic Inquiry* 50 (4): 1097–1111. doi:10.1111/j.1465-7295.2010.00346.x.
stata.com. "var — Vector autoregressive models." Accessed April 24, 2014. www.stata.com/manuals13/tsvar.pdf.
Statistisches Bundesamt. 2012. "Bruttoinlandsprodukt 2011 für Deutschland." Accessed March 22, 2014. https://www.destatis.de/DE/PresseService/Presse/Pressekonferenzen/2012/BIP2011/Pressebroschuere_BIP2011.pdf?__blob=publicationFile.
Stiglitz, Joseph E. 2011. "The media and the crisis: An information theoretic approach." In *Bad news: How America's business press missed the story of the century,* edited by Anya Schiffrin, 22–36. New York: New Press.
Stone, Gerald C., and Maxwell E. McCombs. 1981. "Tracing the time lag in Agenda-Setting." *Journalism & Mass Communication Quarterly* 58 (1): 51–55. doi:10.1177/107769908105800108.

Strömbäck, Jesper. 2008. "Four phases of mediatization: An analysis of the mediatization of politics." *The International Journal of Press/Politics* 13 (3): 228–46. doi:10.1177/1940161208319097.

Strömbäck, Jesper, and Spiro Kiousis. 2010. "A new look at agenda-setting effects--Comparing the predictive power of overall political news consumption and specific news media consumption across different media channels and media types." *Journal of Communication* 60 (2): 271–92. doi:10.1111/j.1460-2466.2010.01482.x.

Tan, Yue, and David H. Weaver. 2013. "Agenda diversity and agenda setting from 1956 to 2004." *Journalism Studies* 14 (6): 773–89. doi:10.1080/1461670X.2012.748516.

Tewksbury, David. 2002. "The role of comparison group size in the third-person effect." *International Journal of Public Opinion Research* 14 (3): 247–63. doi:10.1093/ijpor/14.3.247.

Tewksbury, David, Patricia Moy, and Deborah S. Weis. 2004. "Preparations for Y2K: Revisiting the behavioral component of the third-person effect." *Journal of Communication* 54 (1): 138–55. doi:10.1111/j.1460-2466.2004.tb02618.x.

Tims, Albert R., David P. Fan, and John R. Freeman. 1989. "The cultivation of consumer confidence: A longitudinal analysis of news media influence on consumer sentiment." *Advances in Consumer Research* 16: 758–70.

Trenaman, Joseph, and Denis McQuail. 1961. *Television and the political image: A study of the impact of television on the 1959 general election.* London: Meuthen.

Tversky, Amos, and Daniel Kahneman. 1981. "The framing of decisions and the psychology of choice." *Science* 211 (4481): 453–58. doi:10.1126/science.7455683.

Uhl, Matthias W. 2012. "And action: TV sentiment and the US consumer." *Applied Economics Letters* 19 (11): 1029–34. doi:10.1080/13504851.2011.613739.

Valente, Thomas W. 1993. "Diffusion of innovations and policy decision-making." *Journal of Communication* 43 (1): 30–45. doi:10.1111/j.1460-2466.1993.tb01247.x.

van Dalen, Arjen, Antonis Kalogeropoulus, Helle Møhlgard Svensson, Erik Albæk, and Claes H. de Vreese. 2015. "How mediatized economic news informs the inattentive audience." Re-Inventing Journalism, Winterthur, February 5. http://www.amiando.com/re-inventing-journalism.html;jsessionid=70EAB200A6B28E5DB8F8D1F6D3927545.amiando?page=1148086.

van der Wurff, Richard, Piet Bakker, and Robert G. Picard. 2008. "Economic growth and advertising expenditures in different media in different countries." *Journal of Media Economics* 21 (1): 28–52. doi:10.1080/08997760701806827.

Verbeek, Marno. 2008. *A guide to modern econometrics.* 3rd ed. Chichester: John Wiley & Sons.

Vuchelen, Jef. 2004. "Consumer sentiment and macroeconomic forecasts." *Journal of Economic Psychology* 25 (4): 493–506. doi:10.1016/S0167-4870(03)00031-X.

Wanta, Wayne. 1997. "The messenger and the message: Differences across news media." In *Communication and democracy,* edited by Maxwell E. McCombs, Donald L. Shaw, and David H. Weaver, 137–51. Mahwah, N.J, London: Lawrence Erlbaum.

Wanta, Wayne, and Yu-Wei Hu. 1994a. "The effects of credibility, reliance and exposure on media agenda-setting: A path analysis model." *Journalism Quarterly* 71 (1): 90–98. doi:10.1177/107769909407100109.

———. 1994b. "Time-lag differences in the agenda-setting process: An examination of five news media." *International Journal of Public Opinion Research* 6 (3): 225–40. doi:10.1093/ijpor/6.3.225.

Weaver, David H., Randal A. Beam, Bonnie J. Brownlee, Paul S. Voakes, and G. C. Wilhoit. 2007. *The American journalist in the 21st century: US news people at the dawn of a new millennium.* Mahwah, NJ: Lawrence Erlbaum.

Weischenberg, Siegfried. 1994. "Journalismus als soziales System." In *Die Wirklichkeit der Medien: Eine Einführung in die Kommunikationswissenschaft,* edited by Klaus Merten, Siegfried J. Schmidt, and Siegfried Weischenberg, 427–54. Opladen: Westdeutscher Verlag.

Weischenberg, Siegfried, Martin Löffelholz, and Armin Scholl. 1994. "Merkmale und Einstellungen von Journalisten." *Media Perspektiven* (4): 154–67.
Wilcox, James A. 2007. "Forecasting components of consumption with components of consumer sentiment." *Business Economics* 42 (4): 22–32. doi:10.2145/20070403.
Winter, James P., and Chaim H. Eyal. 1981. "Agenda setting for the civil rights issue." *Public Opinion Quarterly* 45 (3): 376–83. doi:10.1086/268671.
Wooldridge, Jeffrey M. 2009. *Introductory econometrics: A modern approach.* 4th ed. Mason Ohio: South Western cengage learning.
Worlds of Journalism Study. "Sampling instructions." Accessed February 17, 2014. http://www.worldsofjournalism.org/docs/Instructions%20sampling.pdf.
———. 2007. "Master questionnaire: journalists." Accessed February 17, 2014. http://www.worldsofjournalism.org/docs/Master%20questionnaire%20journalists%20EN%20final.pdf.
Wörsdorfer, Sophie. 2005. "Wie die Wirtschaftsberichterstattung der Medien das Konsumentenvertrauen lenkt: Empirische Evidenzen für Deutschland, 1995-2005." *Wirtschaft im Wandel* 11 (11): 338–44. http://www.iwh-halle.de/d/publik/wiwa/11-05.pdf. Accessed December 22, 2010.
Wu, H. D., and Renita Coleman. 2009. "Advancing agenda-setting theory: The comparative strength and new contingent conditions of the two levels of agenda-setting effects." *Journalism & Mass Communication Quarterly* 86 (4): 775–89. doi:10.1177/107769900908600404.
Wu, H. D., Robert L. Stevenson, Hsiao-Chi Chen, and Z. N. Güner. 2002. "The conditioned impact of recession news: A time-series analysis of economic communication in the United States, 1987-1996." *International Journal of Public Opinion Research* 14 (1): 19–36. doi:10.1093/ijpor/14.1.19.
Zaller, John. 1992. *The nature and origins of mass opinion.* Cambridge [England], New York, NY, USA: Cambridge University Press.
Zerback, T., T. Koch, and B. Kramer. 2015. "Thinking of Others: Effects of Implicit and Explicit Media Cues on Climate of Opinion Perceptions." *Journalism & Mass Communication Quarterly* 92 (2): 421–43. doi:10.1177/1077699015574481.
Zubayr, Camille, and Heinz Gerhard. 2005. "Tendenzen im Zuschauerverhalten: Fernsehgewohnheiten und Fernsehreichweiten im Jahr 2004." *Media Perspektiven* (3): 94–104.
———. 2012. "Tendenzen im Zuschauerverhalten: Fernsehgewohnheiten und Fernsehreichweiten im Jahr 2011." *Media Perspektiven* (3): 118–32.
Zucker, Harold G. 1978. "The variable nature of news media influence." In *Communication Yearbook 2*. Vol. 2, edited by Brent D. Rubin, 225–45. New Brunswick, NJ: Transaction Publishers.

Appendix

Table 5: Overview over data, sources and descriptive statistics

	Coun-try	Data source	Ques-tion	Temp. aggr.	Period	Unit of measure (scale)	Descriptive (non-z-standardized data) Min.	Max.	Mean	Stdev.
Objective reality (Non-standardized data are displayed in Lischka and Siegert 2013 (GDP) and Lischka, Kienzler and Mellmann 2014 (adv., sales))										
• GDP	D	Eurostat		Q	Q1 2002 – Q2 2011	m Eur	530'310	646'750	580'716	36'285
• GDP	CH	Eurostat		Q	Q1 2002 – Q2 2011	m Eur	73'074	117'520	85'179	11'916
• Production index (*EI*) (Figure 19)	D	GFSO		M	Jan 2002 – Jun 2011	2010=100	85.6	110.8	97.42	6.9
• Unemployment rate (*EI*) (Figure 20)	D	GFSO		M	Jan 2002 – Jun 2011	Percent	5.9	11.5	8.9	1.51
• Advertising expenditures		NMR								
o Food	D			Q	Q1 1992 – Q4 2009	100m Eur	3.29	4.88	4.27	0.27
o Drinks	D			Q	Q1 1992 – Q4 2009	100m Eur	2.02	2.98	2.58	0.26
o Tobacco	D			Q	Q1 1992 – Q4 2009	100m Eur	0.03	0.29	0.17	0.06
o Health and pharmaceutics	D			Q	Q1 1992 – Q4 2009	100m Eur	1.19	2.12	1.66	0.2
o Textile and clothing	D			Q	Q1 1992 – Q4 2009	100m Eur	0.63	1.03	0.87	0.08
o Shoes and leather	D			Q	Q1 1992 – Q4 2009	100m Eur	0.13	0.29	0.19	0.08
o Automobile	D			Q	Q1 1992 – Q4 2009	100m Eur	3.27	4.92	4.26	0.41
• Sales index		Eurostat								
o Food	D			Q	Q1 1992 – Q4 2009	2005 = 100	63.55	126.12	89.23	16.39
o Drinks	D			Q	Q1 1992 – Q4 2009	2005 = 100	77.34	109.63	97.97	6.25
o Tobacco	D			Q	Q1 1992 – Q4 2009	2005 = 100	67.05	106.93	89.4	9.6
o Health and pharmaceutics	D			Q	Q1 1992 – Q4 2009	2005 = 100	65.74	118.72	84.73	13.35
o Textile and clothing	D			Q	Q1 1992 – Q4 2009	2005 = 100	75.47	162.5	120.06	21
o Shoes and leather	D			Q	Q1 1992 – Q4 2009	2005 = 100	73.24	118.21	105.13	8.81
o Automobile	D			Q	Q1 1992 – Q4 2009	2005 = 100	66.22	117.85	90.56	12.02

Table 5, continued

	Coun-try	Data source	Ques-tion	Temp. aggr.	Period	Unit of measure (scale)	Descriptive (non-z-standardized data) Min.	Max.	Mean	Stdev.
Media-based reality		Media Tenor								
• Total economic news, (Figures 21, 22)										
o *ARD Tagesschau* (1)										
o NT	D			Q	Q1 2002 – Q2 2011	Mean (+1/0/–1)	–0.57	0.15	–0.27	0.16
o NV	D			Q	Q1 2002 – Q2 2011	Abs. no. of reports	66	479	206.68	107.4
o *ZDF heute* (2)										
o NT	D			Q	Q1 2002 – Q2 2011	Mean (+1/0/–1)	–0.56	0.06	–0.29	0.15
o NV	D			Q	Q1 2002 – Q2 2011	Abs. no. of reports	53	529	209.29	120.2
o *RTL aktuell* (3)										
o NT	D			Q	Q1 2002 – Q2 2011	Mean (+1/0/–1)	–0.66	0.12	–0.27	0.16
o NV	D			Q	Q1 2002 – Q2 2011	Abs. no. of reports	41	240	128.39	52.28
o *BILD* (4)										
o NT	D			Q	Q1 2002 – Q2 2011	Mean (+1/0/–1)	–0.53	0.47	–0.17	0.25
o NV	D			Q	Q1 2002 – Q2 2011	Abs. no. of articles	17	360	196.21	103.3
o *SRF Tagesschau*										
o NT	CH			Q	Q1 2007 – Q1 2011	Mean (+1/0/–1)	–0.76	0.64	–0.16	0.36
o NV	CH			Q	Q1 2007 – Q1 2011	Abs. no. of reports	12	350	101.55	95.8
o General economy (1), (2), (3), (4) (Figures 23 – 25)										
o NT	D			M	Jan 2002 – Jun 2011	Mean (+1/0/–1)	–0.91	0.75	–0.18	0.43
o NC	D			M	Jan 2002 – Jun 2011	Stdev. of NT	0.3	1	–0.18	0.15
o NV	D			M	Jan 2002 – Jun 2011	Abs. no. of reports	4	129	36.42	26.1
o Employment (1), (2), (3), (4) (Figures 26 – 28)										
o NT	D			M	Jan 2002 – Jun 2011	Mean (+1/0/–1)	–0.95	0.57	–0.28	0.31
o NC	D			M	Jan 2002 – Jun 2011	Stdev. of NT	0.23	0.94	0.68	0.13
o NV	D			M	Jan 2002 – Jun 2011	Abs. no. of reports	12	112	42.16	19.31

Table 5, continued

	Coun-try	Data source	Ques-tion	Temp. aggr.	Period	Unit of measure (scale)	Descriptive (non-z-standardized data) Min.	Max.	Mean	Stdev.
Social reality										
• Public (Figure 29)		EC CS[1]								
o Expectations for the general economy (*PE*)	D		#1	M	Jan 2002 – Jun 2011	Mean (–100 to +100)[3]	–52.1	21.2	–12.71	16.02
o Expectations for unemployment (*PE*)	D		#2	M	Jan 2002 – Jun 2011	Mean (–100 to +100)[3]	–18.6	71.9	24.02	23.2
o Evaluation of the general economy	D		#3	M	Jan 2002 – Jun 2011	Mean (–100 to +100)[3]	–67.3	29.3	–25.59	27.71
o Financial situation over the next 12 months (FS)	D		#4	M	Jan 2002 – Jun 2011	Mean (–100 to +100)[3]	-11.5	4.2	-3.96	3.59
o Price trends over the next 12 months (PT)	D		#5	M	Jan 2002 – Jun 2011	Mean (–100 to +100)[3]	-18.1	52.9	17.81	14.05
o Evaluation of the right moment to purchase (*RM*)	D		6	M	Jan 2002 – Jun 2011	Mean (–100 to +100)[4]	–30.8	32.2	–7.3	14.62
o Purchase intention (*PI*)	D		7	M	Jan 2002 – Jun 2011	Mean (–100 to +100)[3]	–38.9	–17.9	–28.24	5.04
• Experts (Figures 30, 31)		Ifo WES[2]								
o Evaluations										
o GDP	D		#8	Q	Q1 2002 – Q2 2011	Mean (9/5/1)	1.4	8.8	4.29	2.48
o Investments	D		#9	Q	Q1 2002 – Q2 2011	Mean (9/5/1)	1.2	8.2	4.08	2.47
o Consumption	D		#10	Q	Q1 2002 – Q2 2011	Mean (9/5/1)	1.2	6.6	3.17	1.61
o Expectations										
o GDP	D		#11	Q	Q1 2002 – Q2 2011	Mean (9/5/1)	2.6	8.3	6.17	1.53
o Investments	D		#12	Q	Q1 2002 – Q2 2011	Mean (9/5/1)	2.4	8.1	6.04	1.52
o Consumption	D		#13	Q	Q1 2002 – Q2 2011	Mean (9/5/1)	2.7	7.8	5.96	1.27
o Evaluations										
o GDP	CH		#8	Q	Q1 2002 – Q2 2011	Mean (9/5/1)	1.8	9	5.58	2.2
o Investments	CH		#9	Q	Q1 2002 – Q2 2011	Mean (9/5/1)	1.6	8.8	5.07	2.3
o Consumption	CH		#10	Q	Q1 2002 – Q2 2011	Mean (9/5/1)	3.5	8.7	6.09	1.57
o Expectations										
o GDP	CH		#11	Q	Q1 2002 – Q2 2011	Mean (9/5/1)	2.1	8.7	5.58	1.68
o Investments	CH		#12	Q	Q1 2002 – Q2 2011	Mean (9/5/1)	2.1	8.8	5.47	1.7
o Consumption	CH		#13	Q	Q1 2002 – Q2 2011	Mean (9/5/1)	2.1	7.4	5.04	1.3

Table 5, continued

Notes. GFSO = German Federal Statistical Office. NMR = Nielsen Media Research. M = Monthly, Q = Quarterly temporarily aggregated. Data name abbreviations are equivalent to the ones used in Lischka (2015) except for *NC* (here: *not* inverted standard deviation of *NT*).

1 The Joint Harmonised EU Programme of Business and Consumer Surveys; 2 Ifo World Economic Survey

3 (B) ranging from −100 to +100 on the basis of weighted averages as B = (PP + ½P) – (½M + MM) where PP + P + E + M + MM + N = 100 (N is the percentage of respondents without answer)

4 (B) ranging from −100 to +100 on the basis of weighted averages as B = PP – MM where PP + E + MM + N = 100 (N is the percentage of respondents without answer)

#1 How do you expect the general economic situation in this country to develop over the next 12 months? It will… "get a lot better" (PP), "get a little better" (P), "stay the same," (E) "get a little worse" (M) or "get a lot worse" (MM)

#2 How do you expect the number of people unemployed in this country to change over the next 12 months? The number will… "increase sharply" (PP), "increase slightly" (P), "remain the same," (E) "fall slightly" (M) or "fall sharply" (MM)

#3 How do you think the general economic situation in the country has changed over the past 12 months? It has… "got a lot better" (PP), "got a little better" (P), "stayed the same," (E) "got a little worse" (M) or "got a lot worse" (MM)

#4 How do you expect the financial position of your household to change over the next 12 months? It will…"get a lot better" (PP), "get a little better" (P), "stay the same," (E) "get a little worse" (M) or "get a lot worse" (MM)

#5 By comparison with the past 12 months, how do you expect that consumer prices will develop in the next 12 months? They will… "increase more rapidly" (PP), "at the same rate" (P), "at a slower rate," (E) "stay about the same" (M) or "fall" (MM)

#6 In view of the general economic situation, do you think that now it is the right moment for people to make major purchases such as furniture, electrical/electronic devices, etc.? "yes, it is the right moment now" (PP), "it is neither the right moment nor the wrong moment" (E), "no, it is not the right moment now" (MM)

#7 Compared to the past 12 months, do you expect to spend more or less money on major purchases (furniture, electrical/electronic devices, etc.) over the next 12 months? I will spend… "much more" (PP), "a little more" (P), "about the same" (E), "a little less" (M), "much less" (MM)

#8 This country's general situation regarding overall economy present judgment: "good" (value 9), "satisfactory" (5), "bad" (1)

#9 This country's general situation regarding capital expenditures present judgment: "good" (9), "satisfactory" (5), "bad" (1)

#10 This country's general situation regarding private consumption present judgment: "good" (9), "satisfactory" (5), "bad" (1)

#11 This country's general situation regarding overall economy from now on: expected situation by the end of the next 6 months: "better" (9), "about the same" (5), "worse" (1)

#12 This country's general situation regarding capital expenditures from now on: expected situation by the end of the next 6 months: "better" (9), "about the same" (5), "worse" (1)

#13 This country's general situation regarding private consumption from now on: expected situation by the end of the next 6 months: "better" (9), "about the same" (5), "worse" (1)

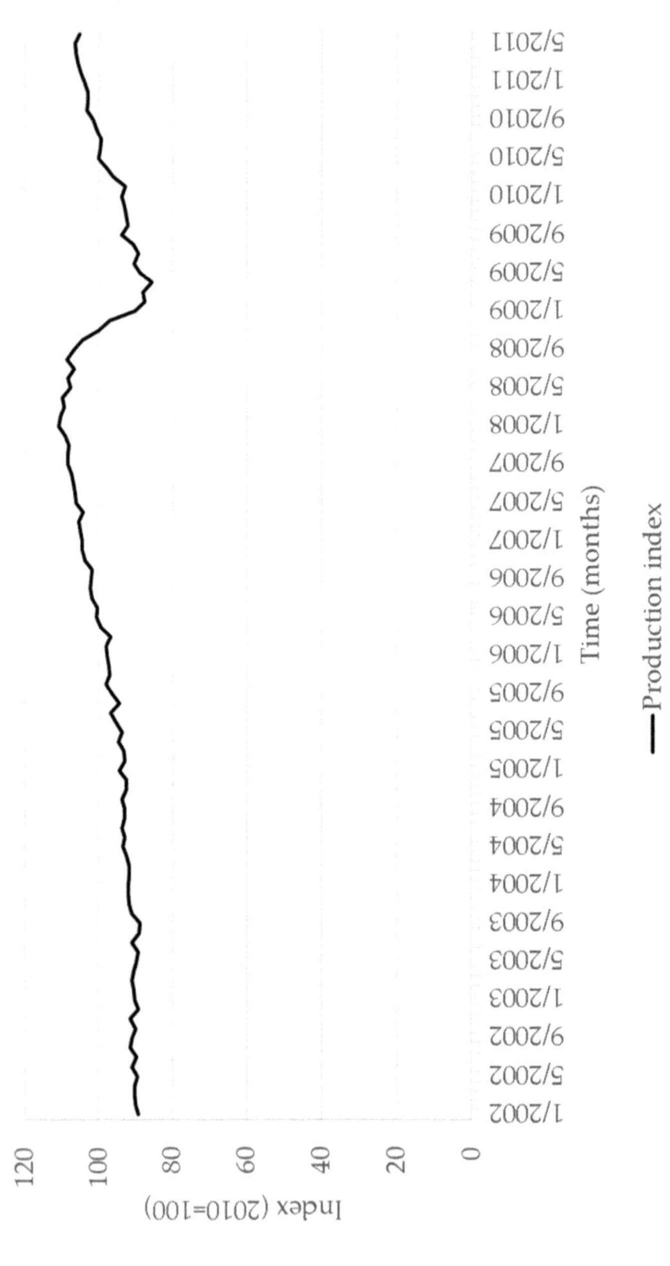

Figure 19: Objective reality: Production index, non-z-transformed data

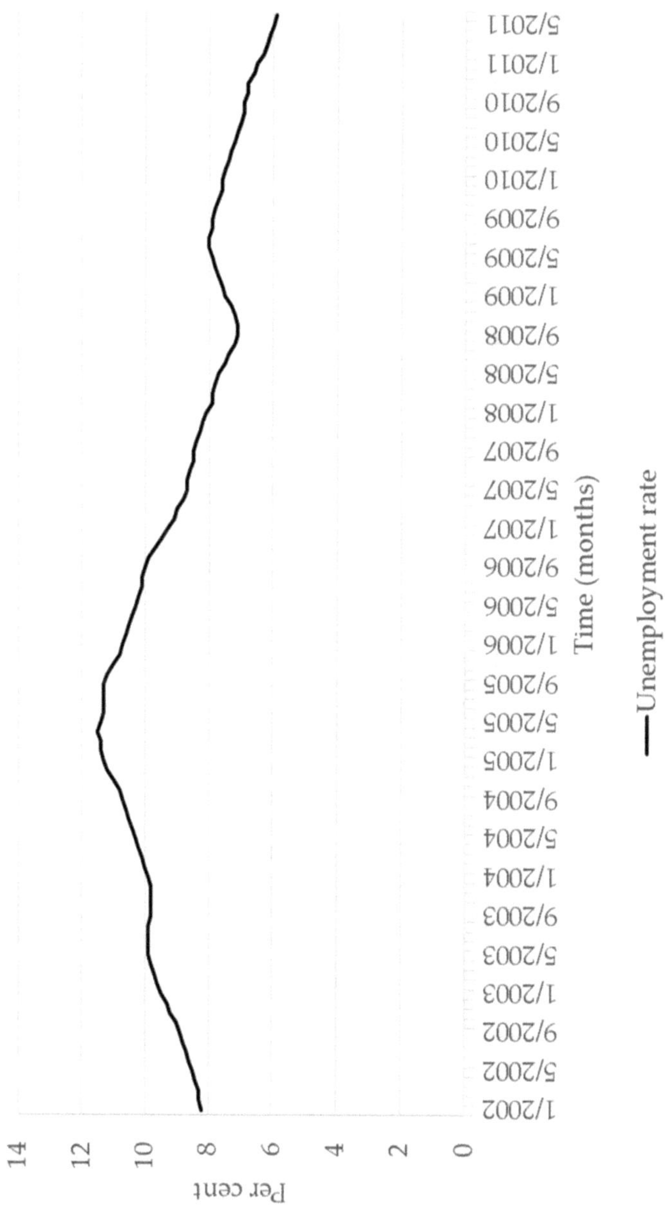

Figure 20: Objective reality: Unemployment rate, non-z-transformed data

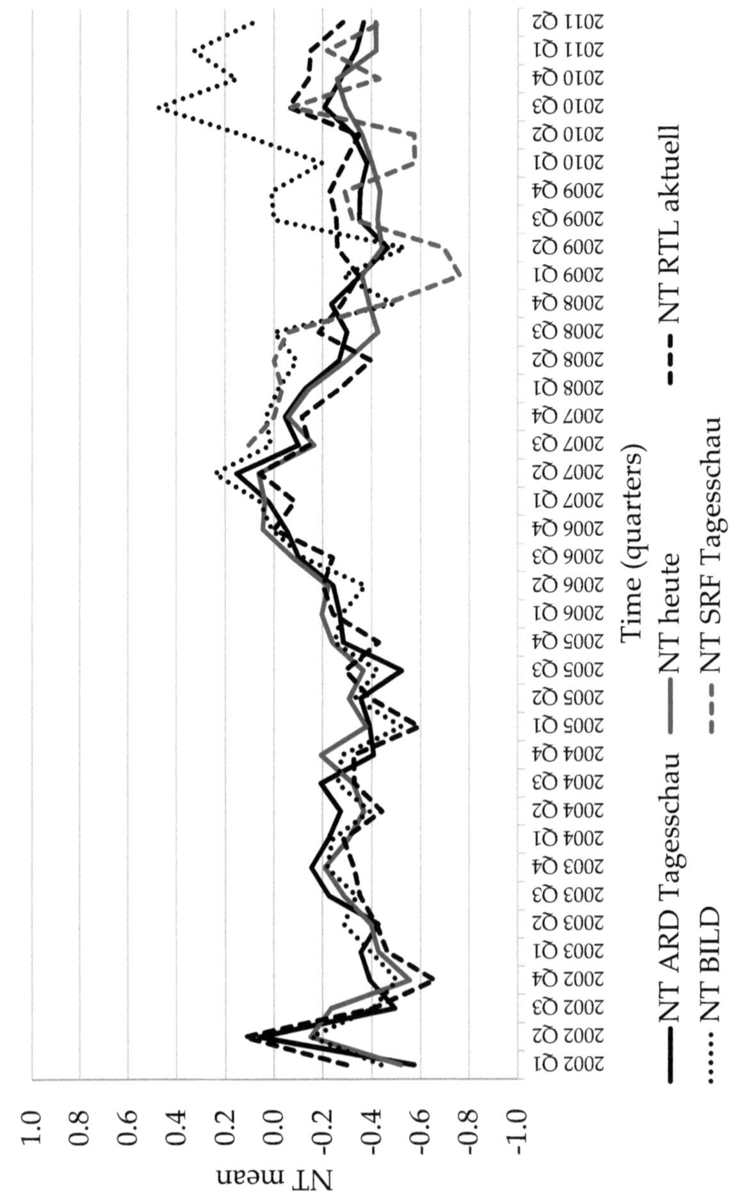

Figure 21: Media-based reality: News tone of total economic news per news outlet, non-z-transformed data

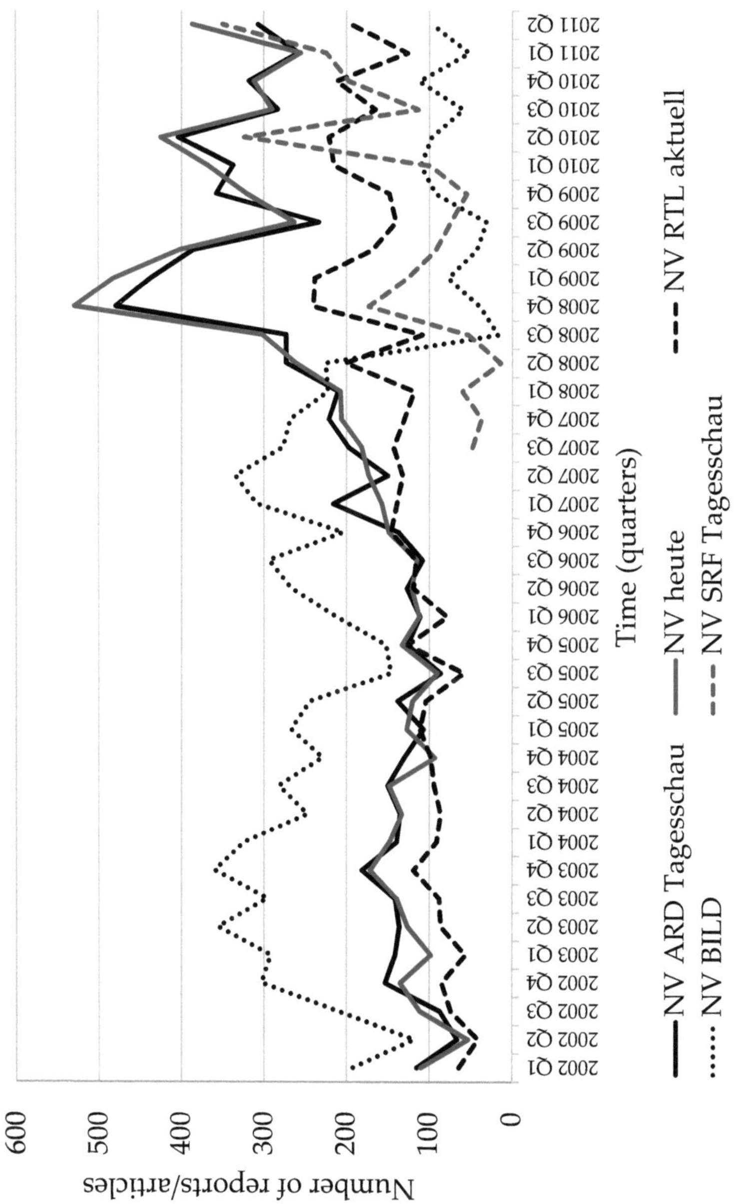

Figure 22: Media-based reality: News volume of total economic news per news outlet, non-z-transformed data

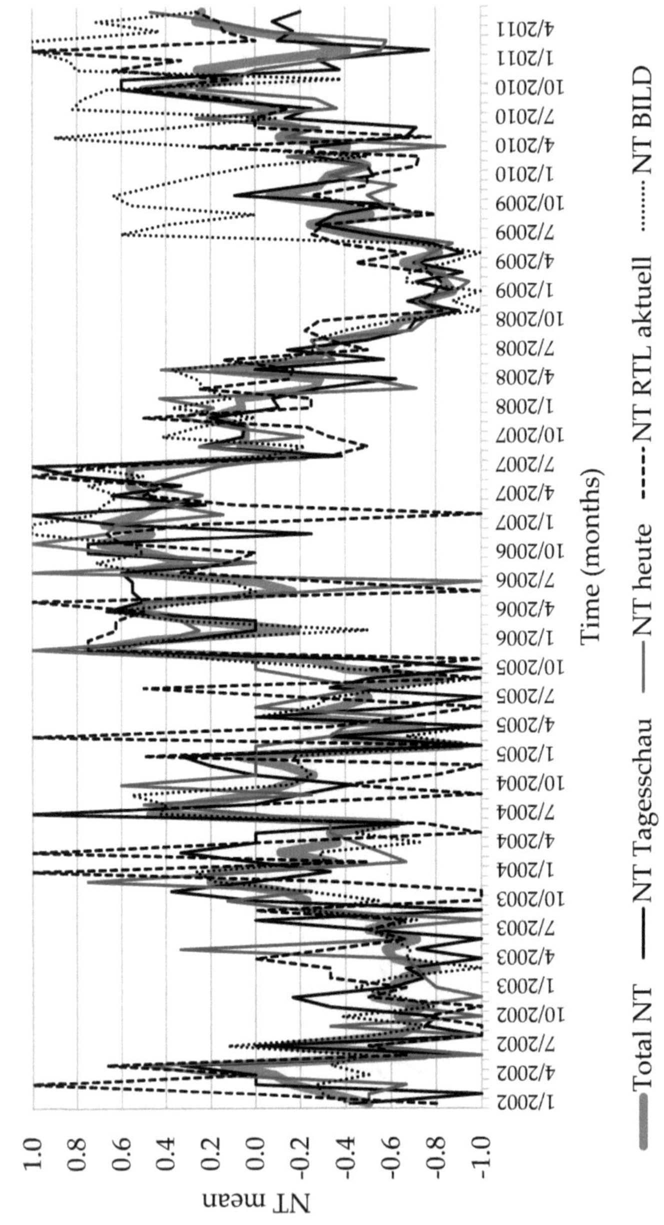

Figure 23: Media-based reality: News tone on the general economy, non-z-transformed data

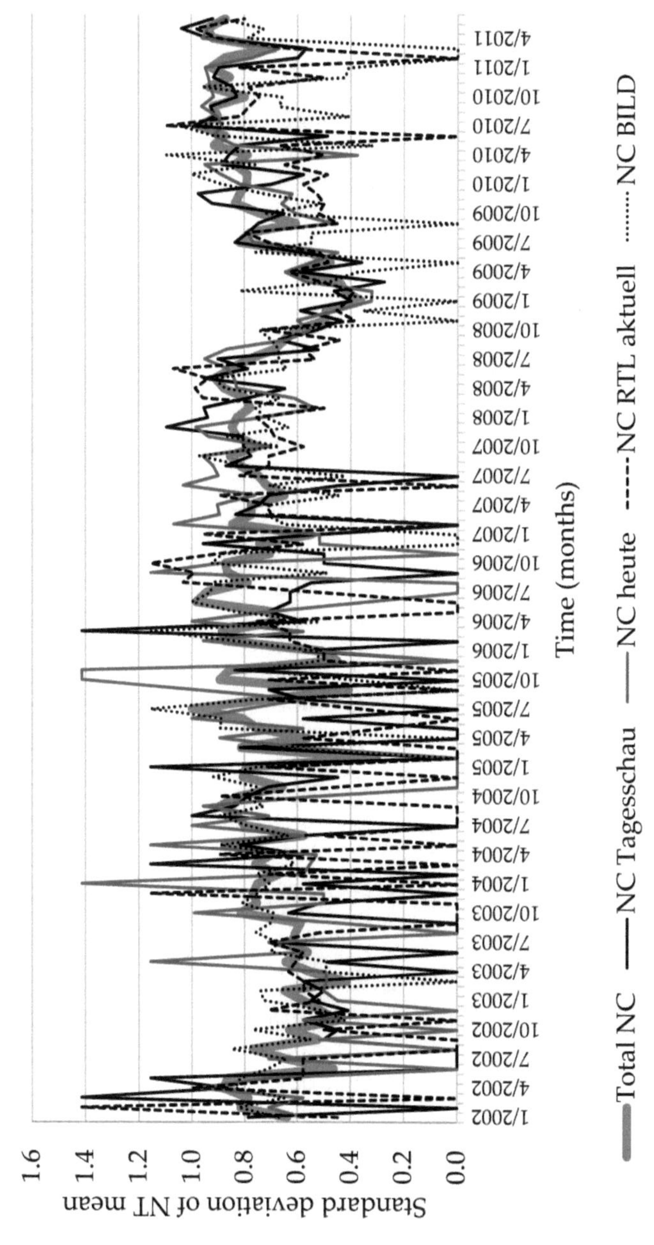

Figure 24: Media-based reality: News tone consonance on the general economy, non-z-transformed data

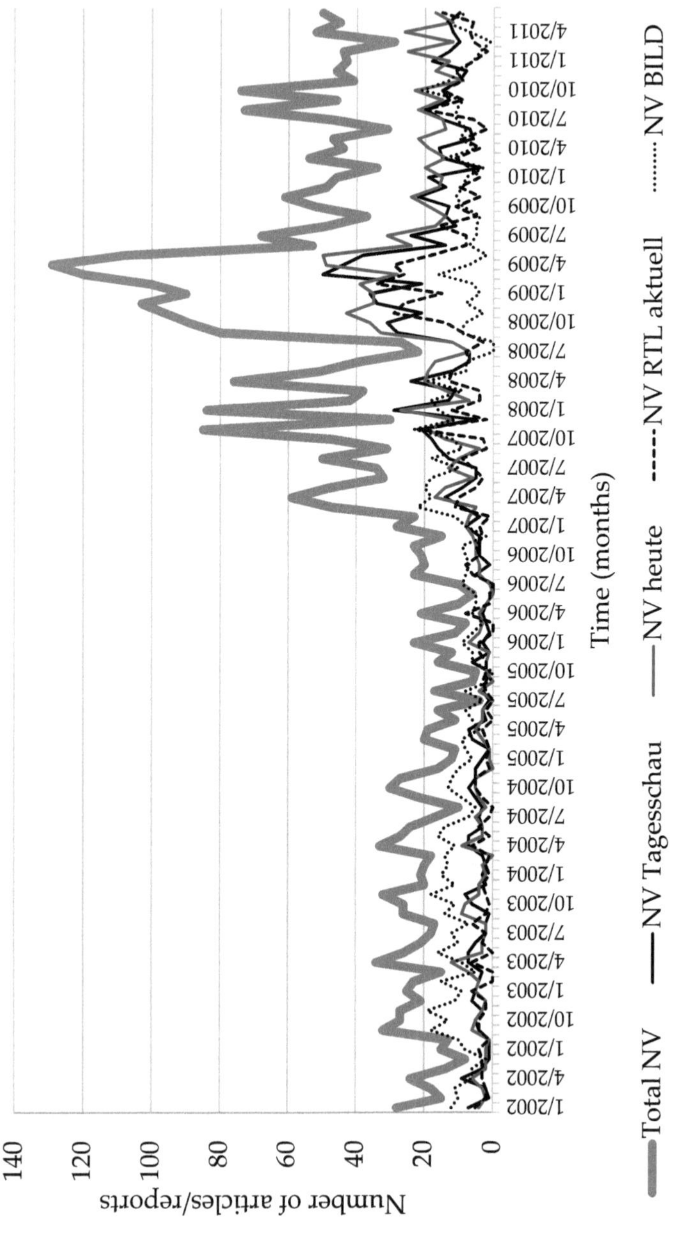

Figure 25: Media-based reality: News volume on the general economy, non-z-transformed data

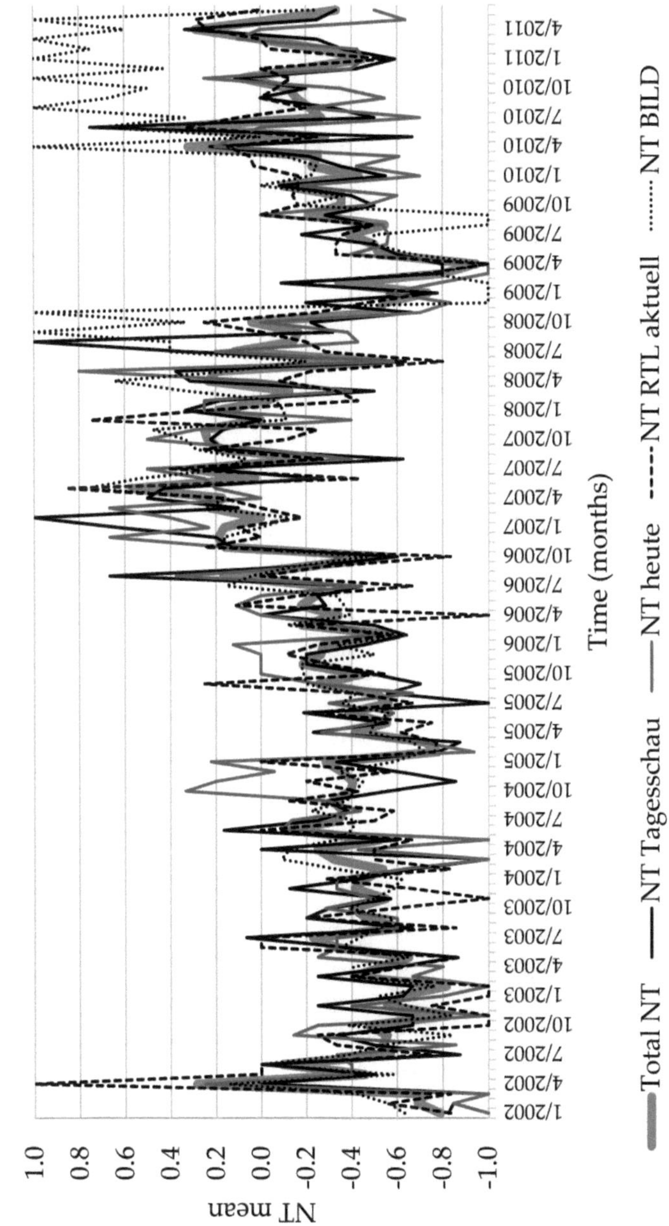

Figure 26: Media-based reality: News tone on employment, non-z-transformed data

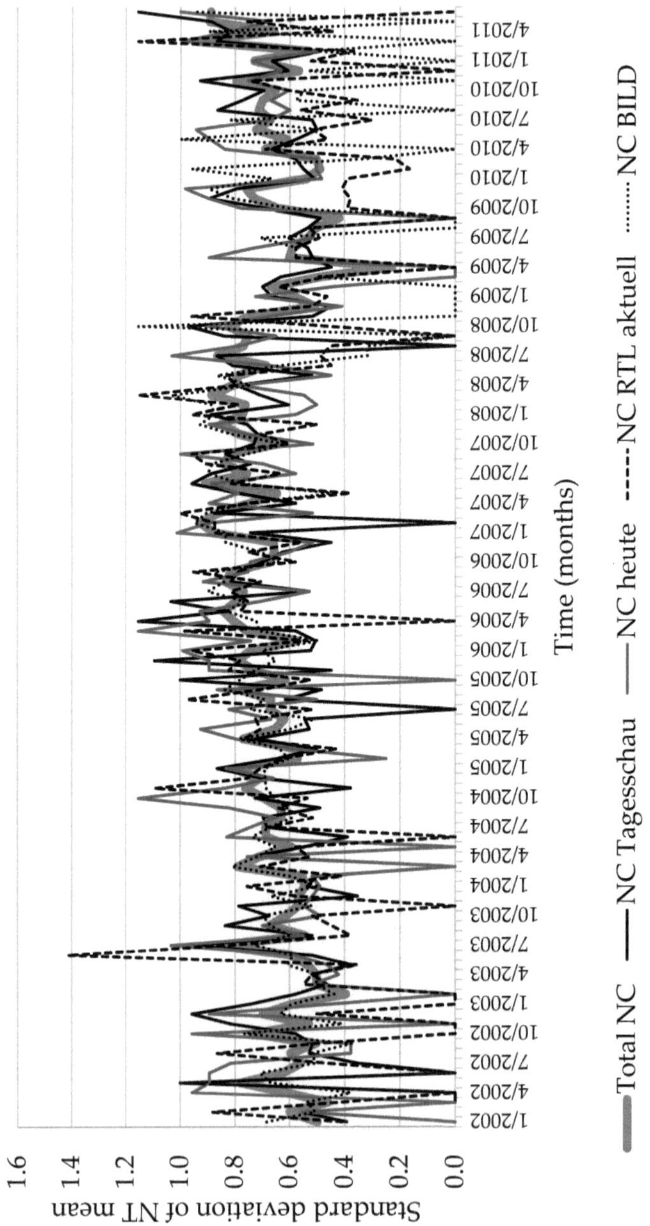

Figure 27: Media-based reality: News tone consonance on employment, non-z-transformed data

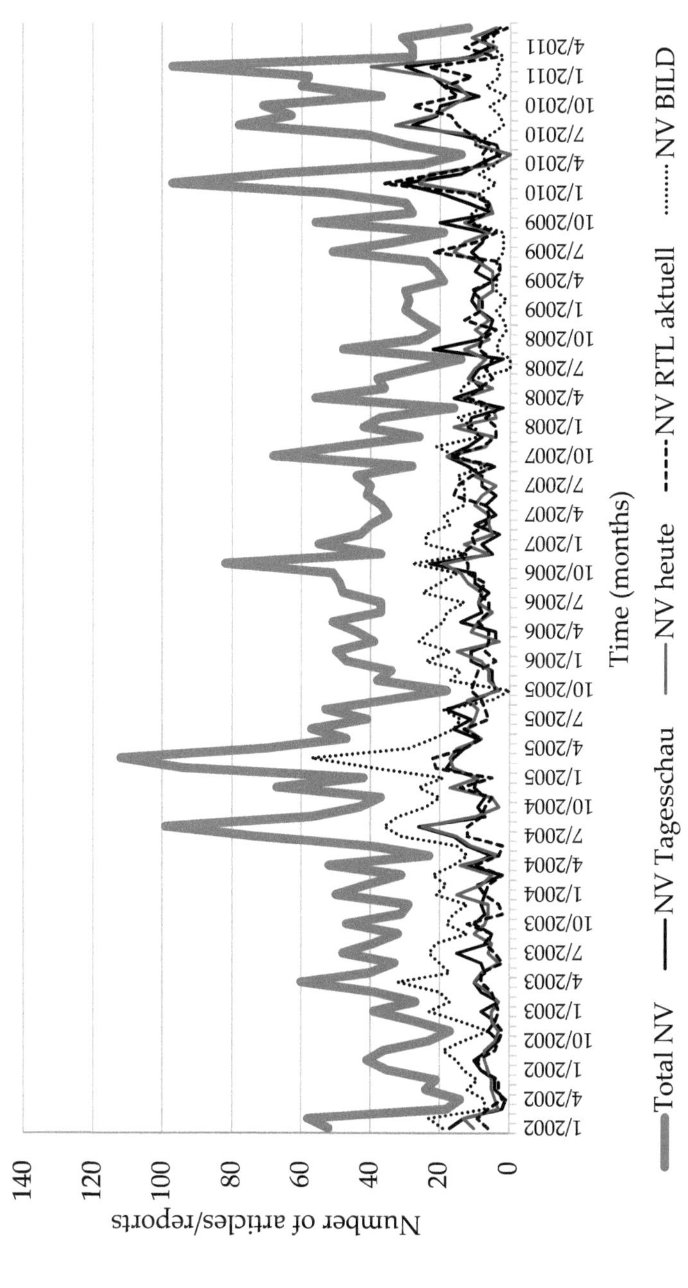

Figure 28: Media-based reality: News volume on employment, non-z-transformed data

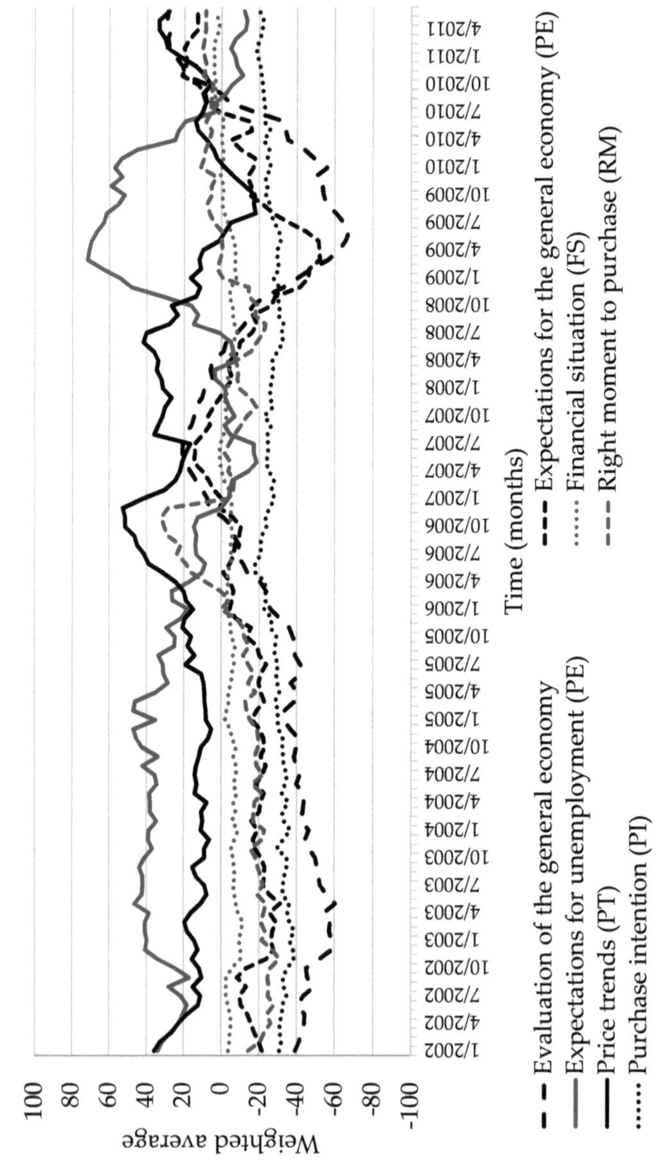

Figure 29: Social reality: Public economic sentiment measured by the EU Programme of Business and Consumer Surveys, non-z-transformed data

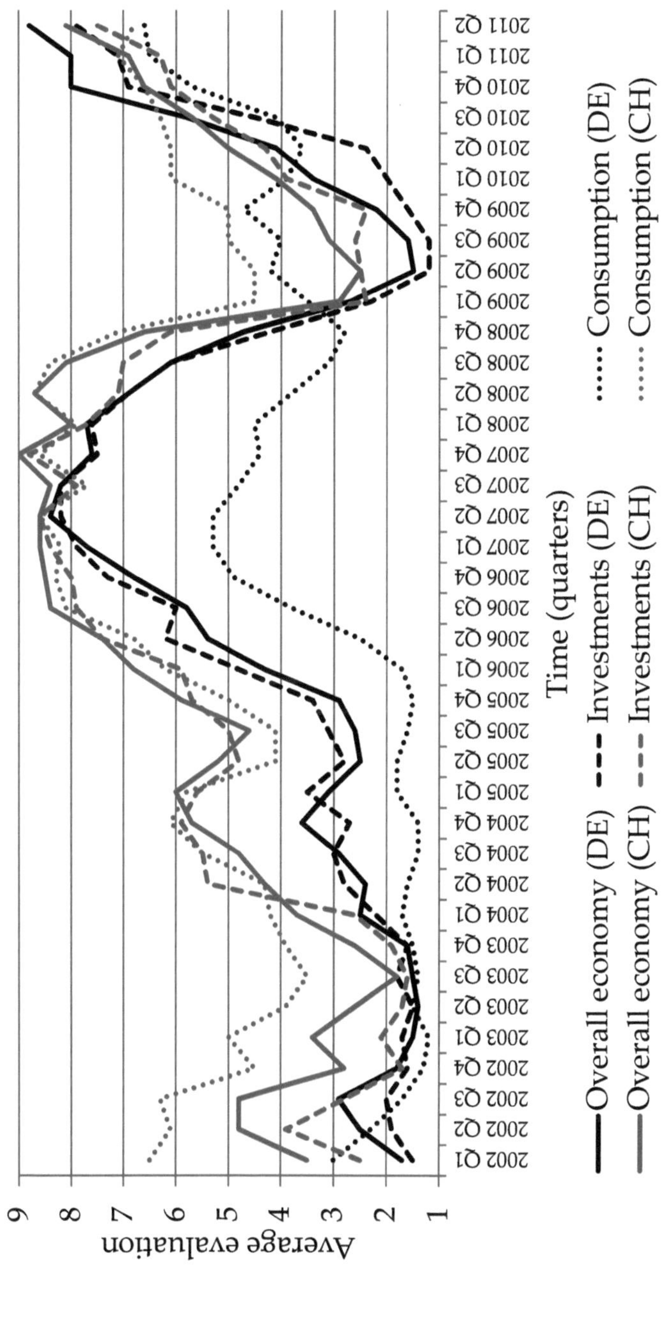

Figure 30: Social reality: Expert economic evaluations measured by the Ifo World Economic Survey, non-z-transformed data

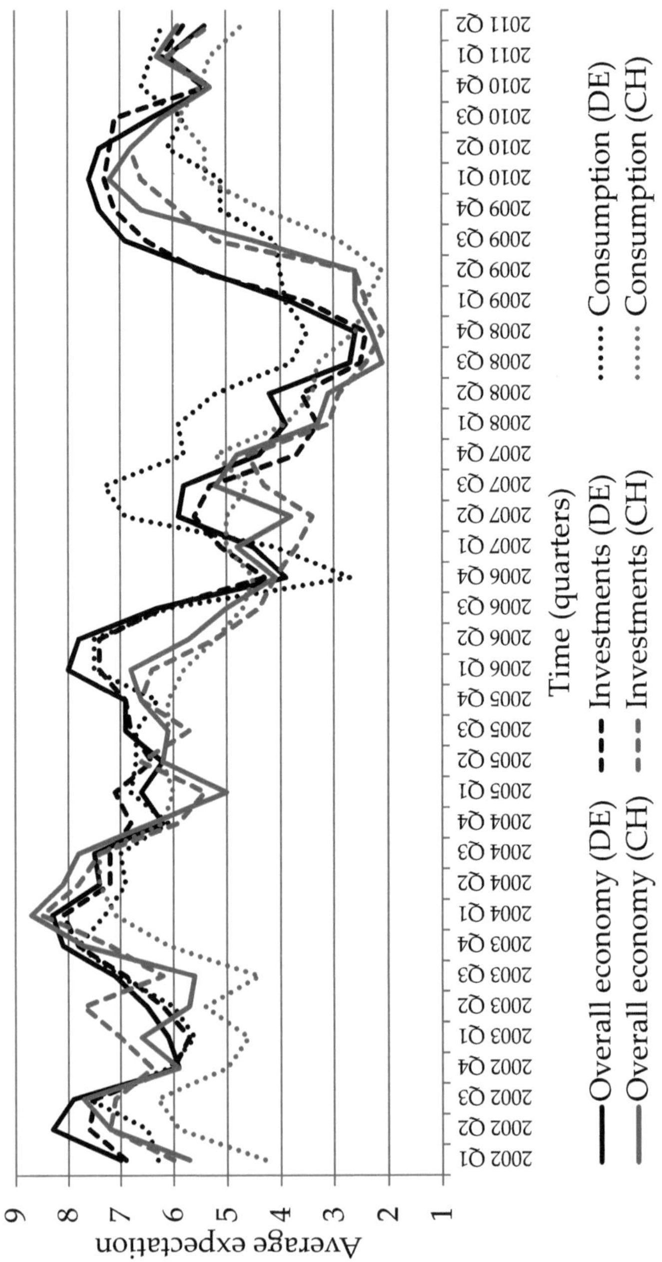

Figure 31: Social reality: Expert economic expectations measured by the Ifo World Economic Survey, non-z-transformed data

Abstracts of associated articles

1. Lischka, Juliane A. 2014. "Different revenue incentives, different content? Comparing economic news before and during the financial crisis in German public and commercial news outlets over time." *European Journal of Communication* 29 (5): 549–66. doi:10.1177/0267323114538851.

   Abstract: This study argues that revenue model incentives determine news content. The goal to make profits and the need to sell audiences to advertisers guides journalistic selection and interpretation and results in commercialized news. We compare the volume, tone, and the obtrusiveness of topics of economic news stories for the German public broadcasters *ARD* and *ZDF*, the commercial broadcaster *RTL*, and the tabloid newspaper *BILD* from 2002-10 (n = 26'467). Results indicate that news selection processes are guided by revenue model incentives since volume and topic of economic news differ across revenue models. News interpretation also depends on the media type.

   Data: Economic news (news topics, tone, consonance, volume) of *ARD Tagesschau, ZDF heute, RTL aktuell, BILD* from 2002 – 2010.

2. Lischka, Juliane A. 2015. "What follows what? Relations between economic indicators, economic expectations of the public, and news on the general economy and unemployment in Germany, 2002–2011." *Journalism & Mass Communication Quarterly,* 92 (2): 374–98. doi:10.1177/1077699015574098.

   Abstract: This study aims to understand dynamic agenda building and agenda setting processes between real-world indicators, public expectations, and aggregated news on the general economy and unemployment for two German public service broadcasters, a commercial broadcaster, and a tabloid newspaper from 2002 to 2011. Vector autoregressive and error correction models and Granger causality tests reveal that (1) news tone relates to real-world indicators, (2) public expectations for the general economy and unemployment are set by the tone of news on the general economy, especially during recession times, and (3) public expectations can forecast the future real-world economy.

Data: Economic news on the general economy and on employment (news tone, consonance, volume) of *ARD Tagesschau, ZDF heute, RTL aktuell, BILD* in total; economic expectations on the general economy and on unemployment development of the general public; production index and unemployment rate; from January 2002 – June 2011.

3. Lischka, Juliane A., and Gabriele Siegert. 2013. "Beeinflussen Wirtschaftsnachrichten auch Wirtschaftserwartungen von Experten? Die Prognosequalität von öffentlich-rechtlichen und Service public Wirtschaftsnachrichten für Erwartungen von Wirtschaftsexperten in Deutschland und in der Schweiz." [Do economic news impact economic expectations of experts? The forecasting quality of public service economic news in Germany and Switzerland.]. *Studies in Communication Sciences* 13 (2): 174–84. doi:10.1016/j.scoms.2013.09.002.

   Abstract: It is possible that economic news not only reports on the economy but also has an impact on the development of an economy by affecting economic expectations. This study explores the impact of economic news on the economic expectations of experts. A content analysis of economic news tone and volume of two German and one Swiss public service news show is combined with survey data on macroeconomic expectations of experts on the topics of the general economy, capital expenditures, and private consumption. Results confirm that past news tone explains up to 70 percent of the variation in economic expectations for private consumption. This effect varies among news shows and the overall economic situation. The authors hold media dependency and an asymmetric third-person effect responsible for these variations.

   Data: Economic news of *ARD Tagesschau, ZDF heute,* and *SRF Tagesschau* (news tone, volume); economic evaluations and expectations of Swiss and German economic experts; Q1 2002 – Q2 2011.

4. Lischka, Juliane A., Stephanie Kienzler, and Ulrike Mellmann. 2014. "Sales drive advertising expenditures: Evidence for consumer packaged and durable goods in Germany." *International Journal of Marketing Studies* 6 (1): 31–44. doi:10.5539/ijms.v6n1p31.

Abstract: The relation between sales and advertising is both complex and diverse. Whether advertising activities drive or follow sales is still unclear. We uncover this relation distinguishing between consumer packaged goods (CPG) and durable consumer goods (DCG) industries. We fit vector autoregressive models to sales and advertising expenditures of four CPG and three DCG industries in Germany from 1991 q1 to 2009 q4. Findings reveal that advertising expenditures do not increase total sales of industries according to the distribution hypothesis. According to the deterministic view, advertising budgeting is often influenced by previous sales and partly by future sales expectations. We conclude that past sales and partly sales expectations may change company and marketing goals that eventually affect the use of strategic communication instruments such as advertising.

Data: Advertising expenditures and sales of four non-durable and three durable goods industries, Q1 1991 – Q4 2009.

Author biography and affiliation

Juliane A. Lischka is a Senior Research and Teaching Assistant at the Media Economics & Management division at the Institute of Mass Communication and Media Research, University of Zurich, Switzerland. She holds a Ph.D. in Media and Mass Communication Studies from the University of Zurich, Switzerland, a M.A. and B.A. in Media and Mass Communication Studies from the Friedrich Schiller University Jena, Germany. She was Visiting Doctoral Fellow at the Media Management and Transformation Centre, Jönköping International Business School, Jönköping University, Sweden, a Visiting Fellow at the Reuters Institute for the Study of Journalism, University of Oxford, UK, and a Visiting Fellow at the School of Journalism, Media and Cultural Studies, Cardiff University, UK.

Her fields of research focus on (1) media effects on society, i.e., the role of economic news in private and corporate economic opinion formation and decision making, (2) media economics and management, i.e., news media organizations' responses to challenges and opportunities of the digital age, as well as (3) effects of the Internet usage on society, i.e., the role of digital surveillance, big data, and online social network algorithms for journalism and society.

Institute of Mass Communication and Media Research, University of Zurich, Switzerland, Andreasstrasse 15, 8050 Zurich, Switzerland;
Email: j.lischka@ipmz.uzh.ch; Twitter: @JulianeLischka

MIX
Papier aus verantwortungsvollen Quellen
Paper from responsible sources
FSC® C105338

If you have any concerns about our products,
you can contact us on
ProductSafety@springernature.com

In case Publisher is established outside the EU,
the EU authorized representative is:
Springer Nature Customer Service Center GmbH
Europaplatz 3, 69115 Heidelberg, Germany

Printed by Libri Plureos GmbH
in Hamburg, Germany